A STROKE WAS MY TEACHER

A Stroke Was My Teacher

JAMES G. CRAWFORD PhD

*"We earn our living by how we provide for our families.
We earn our life by how we provide for strangers."*

A message from the Spirit

Common Sense Rules for Stroke and Heart Attack Survival (S & HA)

1. Every S and HA is an oxygen emergency and is a water emergency.
2. Your body extracts fluid from your tissues at nighttime causing dehydration.
3. Most strokes and heart attacks occur before noon.
4. Your blood is at its point of highest concentration before noon. Concentrated blood is most likely to form blockages to brain and heart thus S & HA.
5. The stress hormone cortisol is at its peak level before noon and causes blood vessel constriction contributing to blockage.
6. We lose our sense of thirst and our magnesium, a sticky cell mediator, as we age.

The Solution

1. Drink a full glass of hot water immediately upon arising and at least two extra quarts per day.
2. Ask your doctor for magnesium supply recommendation.
3. Ask your doctor for cortisol recommendation.
4. Avoid all sugar as high blood sugar also causes blood to thicken. The major causes of death among diabetics are HA & S.

BALBOA.
PRESS
A DIVISION OF HAY HOUSE

ISBN: 978-1-4525-3567-8 (sc)
ISBN: 978-1-4525-3568-5 (e)
ISBN: 978-1-4525-3569-2 (hc)
Library of Congress Control Number: 2011909991

Balboa Press books may be ordered through booksellers or by contacting:

Balboa Press
A Division of Hay House
1663 Liberty Drive
Bloomington, IN 47403
www.balboapress.com
1-(877) 407-4847

Because of the dynamic nature of the Internet, any web addresses or links contained in
this book may have changed since publication and may no longer be valid. The views
expressed in this work are solely those of the author and do not necessarily reflect the
views of the publisher, and the publisher hereby disclaims any responsibility for them.

The author of this book does not dispense medical advice or prescribe the use of any
technique as a form of treatment for physical, emotional, or medical problems without the
advice of a physician, either directly or indirectly. The intent of the author is only to offer
information of a general nature to help you in your quest for physical, emotional and spiritual
wellbeing. In the event you use any of the information in this book for yourself, which is your
constitutional right, the author and the publisher assume no responsibility for your actions.

Any people depicted in stock imagery provided by Fotosearch are models,
and such images are being used for illustrative purposes only.
Certain stock imagery © Fotosearch.

Printed in the United States of America

Balboa Press rev. date: 7/18/2011

KEY TOPICS

DEDICATION

This book is dedicated to all souls who practice the truth that,
as Einstein once explained,
"Foolish faith in authority is the worst enemy of truth."

My Heroes

- Fereydoon Batmanghelidj—for his intuitive insight on the effect of dehydration on many disease processes.

- Richard Bernstein—for his incredible intuitive insights on the process of diabetes.

- David Brownstein—for his intuitive insight on the effect of iodine on breast cancer.

- Albert Einstein—for his intuitive insights on human nature.

- Albert Sabin—for his remarkable intuitive insight that sugar consumption distinguished countries with polio epidemics from countries with no polio epidemics.

Table of Contents

PART 1 A STROKE WAS MY TEACHER

Chapter One Purposes Of Book   3

Chapter Two How The Odyssey Began   16

Chapter Three Proposed Stroke And Heart Attack Mechanisms

24

List Of Illustrations

Tables

FOREWORD

Jim Crawford is a scientific colleague and personal friend of mine for a couple of decades. He is a maverick who does not march to the drummer that everybody follows. He is his own drummer. Accordingly his approach to science and medicine is quite unorthodox which is reflected in his quote of Einstein, "Foolish faith in authority is the worst enemy of truth". I can add to that declaration by saying that one should have the courage to question "established" dogmas. No progress can be made without questioning dogmas. George Bernard Shaw, the Irish writer, said "The reasonable man tries to adapt himself to the world. The unreasonable one persists in trying to adapt the world to himself. *Therefore all progress depends on the unreasonable man.*" (Emphasis mine.) Remember that advances in molecular biology were made by questioning the central dogma that existed with the basic premise, "DNA makes RNA makes Protein". That dogma was shattered when RNA viruses (also known as retroviruses) and reverse transcriptase were discovered in the process of explaining non-standard behavior of cellular machinery. The same is true for the new and developing field of Epigenetics wherein heritable changes in phenotype are caused by mechanisms other than changes in underlying DNA codon sequence. One has to search for remedies for certain diseases outside the traditional thinking path. The diesel engine was designed and produced by General Motors (and not by the railroad companies which insisted on using steam engines forever) and became the standard in modern railroad.

In this monograph Dr. Crawford has assembled a bunch of biochemical agents and mechanistic pathways and tried to weave a tapestry to make sense of certain biochemical phenomena leading to stroke. It may appear that he is going out on a limb. However, some of the explanations he is offering deserve a hard look by medical researchers. When he started to write the monograph it was intended as a primer ("do's and don'ts") for would-be stroke victims. In the course of writing it he saw "the woods among the trees" and subsequently developed a comprehensive mechanism for the incidence of stroke. There are some factors which trigger clot formation while others propagate and precipitate the event. Dehydration characterized by hypovolemia resulting in concentration of cellular and molecular entities in blood, is the principal mechanism in his hypothesis. I consider that hypothesis deserves serious consideration in any further study by the medical research community. Dehydration can contribute to increasing the fibrinogen (the precursor for fibrin in a blood clot) concentration and coupled with Magnesium deficiency (which can enhance platelet aggregation) could induce clot formation. Once the clot travels further in the circulatory system then stroke and heart attack follow. In this respect this monograph (especially the schematics he has proposed for the occurrence of stroke) is a "must-read" for cardiovascular researchers studying the etiology of heart attack and stroke in order to validate or refute Crawford's hypothesis. Some epidemiological studies bear out some premises of his hypothesis.

The bold challenge that Crawford presents against the prevailing causative mechanism for stroke being atrial fibrillation held by the medical community is worth a serious evaluation in view of the disproportionate relationship between the incidence of atrial fibrillation and the occurrence of stroke. His suggestion of addressing other causative factors while not excluding atrial fibrillation appears to be sound.

As for the Neuropathy hypothesis he relies on anecdotal events (Post-Polio syndrome or the nexus between statins and neuro-muscular debility) rather than evidence-based results. While a pre-sensitized tissue could manifest new insult upon exposure to certain agents no solid evidence is currently available to support it. That should not deter the researchers from testing the hypothesis. The shingles outbreak later in life once someone is exposed to chicken pox in early childhood is one example in this regard, although it is a lingering virus and not a new agent that causes the eruption. However, I feel that homeopathic treatment ("like cures like") runs counter to the neuropathy hypothesis that Crawford promotes which needs to be properly reconciled in any study design.

Part 2 of the monograph reads like an autobiography (of course restricted to the post-stroke period). Crawford apparently kept a meticulous record of his physiological and anatomical changes caused by the stroke. He narrates his personal experience over a course of 3 years after the stroke and describes the various treatment regimens (conventional as well as newer techniques). Such cataloging is very helpful for would-be stroke victims in managing their post-stroke life if not helping them avoid a stroke incident. He gives some prescriptions for avoiding a secondary stroke attack such as: (1) kicking the sugar habit, (2) drinking plenty of water as one of the daily activities (whether thirsty or not), and (3) taking certain supplements like antioxidants, among others, to maintain proper health.

This monograph should rekindle efforts in the medical research community to reexamine the fundamental cause of stroke and heart attack and suggest preventive measures to avoid a stroke or a heart attack. Besides, this would also be an interesting manual for future stroke victims who can gain from the experience of a stroke patient who has taken the trouble to delve deep into the causative factors of stroke and developing a regimen for the management of post-stroke life. It is my pleasure to commend this work of "blood and sweat, and intellectual toil" to all concerned about their health.

Sethuraman Subramanian
Wake Forest, North Carolina
February 19, 2011

PROLOGUE

The original intent of this book was to record my understanding and experience in having an embolic stroke. It soon became evident that before I could offer a meaningful interpretation of my experience, I needed to first determine the status of the present footings of vascular research in general.

While trying to get a grip on some of the mysteries within that arena, I decided to try to develop a unifying interpretation for how the two most lethal diseases—heart attack (HA) and stroke (S)—are related. Thus, this book focuses mostly on a new concept to explain the relationship between these two diseases and why they are positioned within the three top disease problems worldwide (the third being cancer).

The first part of the book, in chapter form is concerned with the science of stroke, while the second part of the book is in lesson form with my experience, understanding, and suggestions for managing embolic stroke.

In contrast to the publishers/authors of most technical books that forbid the use of their work without permission, let me say simply this: this book is a product of my study now into its fourth year, and I consider it my volunteer work and gift to humanity. Anyone who can find a way to use portions of this book to promote understanding of new concepts of stroke, heart attack, neurologic diseases, and all other maladies driven by dehydration, is free and encouraged to use my material for educational purposes. Of course, appropriate citation to and credit for the source is expected, and I would appreciate knowing what and where material was used by e-mail to estroke911@gmail.com. The use of any portion of this book to generate personal gain is specifically prohibited. There will be no financial gain associated with this effort.

Also please note if this book should become a significant source of revenue, my intention is to donate the majority of profit to two church-affiliated colleges–Alma College and Brevard College. Success for this book is driven by my life-long interest in promoting the educational process.

I have purposefully used a self-publishing vehicle so I would not be encumbered by publisher restrictions.

Excuse me now, I've got to hustle—I'm 81 and would really like to finish these projects before I reach 112.

—James Crawford

ACKNOWLEDGMENTS

Acknowledgments are in the past tense for historical reason, and for some, because I do not know their mortal state. I do know this will be accurate sooner or later. Each of the named probably unknowingly had influence on the preparation of the manuscript.

Thanks are due to my golfing buddies from Terre Haute, Indiana, Dr. Tom Conway MD, Walt Kindrick, Charles Uhl, Pete Farmer, and Tom Kelly. Each was the definition of a perfect gentleman, and how I got confused with those of that character, I shall never know.

In the great friends category was Erwin Mosher of Mason, Michigan, an all-around great guy; Dick Stuckey of Alma, Michigan, it's an enigma as to how a moral pillar of his stature found common ground with me, but it was much appreciated.

Thanks to Dr. Don Carpenter MD, whose ability to cut to the center of an issue with frightening clarity and precision was always appreciated.

Dr. Sethuraman Subramanian PhD, a helpful, longtime colleague who helped immeasurably on the technical aspect of this work, invoking his acid tests with reckless abandon.

Dr. Pete Peterson MD, a gentleman and a scholar who had encyclopedic knowledge of music, both classical and jazz, and was an authority on aircraft and their history. He was the essence of kindness and a model of the best human qualities. Pete was teamed with his wife Marge, who in her own right had the enviable capacity to make her point in six words or less (it seemed to me).

Acknowledgment of the mother of our children, Ernestene, is made to recognize her as a teacher of how to overcome adversity. Also note is made of my colleague Ted Dayhuff of Terre Haute, Indiana, who taught us how to pass gracefully from this life.

Finally, I give credit and honor to my wife Sylvia, who still teaches the virtue of patience and how to live successfully with a guy in overdrive.

Most grateful thanks to all. I am not the first author to observe that it takes a village to write a book. As I subscribe to that view, I want to acknowledge some of the members of my village: Some of the people named above did not know they contributed to this effort.

Friends who responded to my request to critically evaluate the book in terms of content, clarity, and organization include Fred Greene, who almost single-handedly suggested a book strategy that demanded a total rewrite, something that only a former state prison warden would know how to accomplish with dignity and force. Also to be noticed are David and Joyce Gibbs. Also, reader Ruth Crawford—"motivator in chief" for her students—with an eye for why.

Reader John Dreier (known to his friends as Herr Dreier) and his son Richie contributed to file management. They offered valuable text changes that replaced confusion with clarity and helped transform a complicated schematic into an understandable flow chart. Well done, guys!

Reader Dave Kersey, an accomplished CEO, who could spot a written weakness faster than a speeding participle.

I must thank friends who are master librarians and authorities on book structure. What skilled villagers we have in Annette Blum and Dave Eden.

Science-oriented professionals include Dr. Richard Dardas PhD, a former Pfizer colleague who teamed with me to make many biomedical discoveries.

Dr. Jim May PhD, a former college professor at the Citadel, was someone with an appreciation for the hard work required in creating a useful book.

Of Dr. Sethuraman Subramanian, I can say honestly that if ever you needed the eye of an eagle coupled with the wisdom of an English-speaking Solomon, this villager is your man. Also a former Pfizer colleague, his insight and crisp problem-solving makes for a strong friend. Sub is a published authority and interpreter of Hindu text, among his many talents. It is a privilege to count Sub and his wife Ana as friends, along with their highly accomplished daughters Sumi, Suki, and Mekhala.

Library- and book-oriented professionals include Kathleen Barnes, Cindy Bird, Annette Blum, Kathleen Schmieder, and Ruby Sprouse. Ruby, drawing on her college teaching career, utilizing MS Word 2010 and her graphics skills, made major contributions to the text and cover design, allowing us to bring the project to the finish line in record time. Great job, Ruby. Friends who cultivate spirit-driven life and love are Pattie Beggs and Coral Thorsen.

SPECIAL THANKS

I Now Know Why We Have Four-letter Words

Special thanks are due to Cindy Bird; she has taken pieces of a complex manuscript and translated, fashioned, and formatted them into a readable document. Her special skills using Microsoft Word are the difference between total frustration and calm resolution of intent for a novice. Cindy transformed an endless task laced with confusion into a completed project. Thanks seem hardly adequate.

As for four-letter words, Cindy's maximum expression of discontent with outcome is her term, "Dag nab it!" This expression simply takes too long to utter for the impatient such as me, when a word like *golf* (for example) is available—and is quicker. Nonetheless, I offer super thanks to my superhero.

Couldn't have done it without you.

—Dr. Jim

PERMISSIONS GRANTED

1. Krispin N. Sullivan
   "Magnesium Update." Nutrition and Health: Essential Nutrients for Health Maintenance and Prevention and Reversal of Disease Processes. Krispin Sullivan, MS, CN, 7 Sept. 1998. Web. 23 Feb. 2011. <http://krispin.com/magnes.html>.

2. Dr. David Brownstein
   Iodine Why You Need It—why you can't live without it
   Medical Alternatives Press, Bloomfield, Michigan
   For further information, please go to www.drbrownstein.com

3. John Kehoe
   Mind Power into the 21st Century
   Zoetic, Inc., British Columbia, Canada

PART ONE

A Stroke Was My Teacher

CHAPTER ONE

Purposes Of Book

Introduction

This book was written not to convince anyone of anything, rather to show how it is possible to look at some of the data others have seen, and then through that effort, how one can be lead to a different conclusion. For this account of stroke and heart attack, the roots of this path of thought can be traced back to the Framingham study that originated in 1947, and continues today 50 years later.

A Stroke was my Teacher is offered to that category of the population who takes responsibility for their own health, and chooses to look beyond the offerings of the traditional approach to medical practice. Readers attracted to this book are proactive and usually challenge medical dogma and our national sense that medical success is defined as management of symptoms.

In this book, you will find many of the details for what it is like to experience and then try to manage and understand the effects of an embolic stroke. Within this record of events as they happened, may be found results and assessment of numerous stroke-treatments. These include modalities recognized for stroke, and those only recommended by product merchants. I have discussed what has been helpful to me, and what has not. An important goal for this book is to tell you what steps you can start today to minimize risk/prevent these vascular events from occurring. Also discussed is what to do if you have already had a warning stroke.

This account is presented from the perspective of a life-long career in medical science from graduate school at the University of Michigan, through 37 years of research at NIH and the Pfizer Corp.

This book was written for general public consumption as a handbook on what to expect from the experience. It was also written for use by vascular scientists who are willing to look at stroke and heart attack through a lens not colored by accepted medical dogma.

Book Strategy

I have referred to a quote throughout my entire career that captures my sense of the definition of a scientist. From memory I believe it was Compte de Denois who stated something to the effect that, "A scientist is a person who can look at what everyone else looks at but sees what no one else has seen".

As for strategy, there are two important aspects of this work of which the reader should be aware. One, the contents of this book as assembled, have not been the subject of peer review, and thus have not received scrutiny by vascular research authorities. I have left it up to the reader to decide if what I have said makes sense. What it does offer are supporting references for my story which themselves were subjected to peer review, and thus are considered valid. Where I have discussed my theories that represent a new interpretation of existing scientific records, I have clearly identified those sections of the book with the word **Hypothesis** or **Theory** in the title. This is especially notable in the book section where I have discussed the mechanisms for stroke (S) and heart attack (HA), which appear as a flow chart. I consider this a new look at old data for addition to future stroke literature if proven true.

One clear message I learned while working at Pfizer was that a research guy is not a welcome guest when entering the domain of a production department. I found out that offering unsolicited evidence for a new understanding of an old production method was a prescription for personal grief and a source of embarrassment for the resident engineers. I am again faced with that potential problem here as well, by entering the domain of highly qualified vascular research talent with a 50-year history, when out of the blue, a nobody from nowhere announces "Hey guys, have you thought of looking at atrial fibrillation (A Fib) in this light? Have you ever considered that A Fib may simply be the way our bodies announce the presence of an inflammatory agent. Is it possible one lesson here is first a plea to not waste science to look for something to mask the symptom, but rather to use science to find out why excess cortisol (as one possible inflammatory agent) became elevated in the first place?"

All I can say is, I am only trying to be helpful, and who knows, maybe there is something here worthy of study. After 50 years of close attention, vascular diseases are still among the top killers worldwide, so it is not as if we have all of the answers. Maybe it will take radical ideas to help reset research objectives.

My approach to uncovering and formulating new ideas about S and HA is one in which I reviewed relevant published reports and showed how some of those reports could be interpreted to support my theory of S and HA mechanisms. As for this book, its backbone consists of showing how S and HA could be related to hydration status. Here a case is made that dehydration, coupled with numerous other possible cofactors could account for clot formation that leads to S and HA. This thesis suggests that atrial fibrillation, while recognized as a risk factor for those diseases, is more likely a statistical matter of guilt by association rather than anything causative when viewed in the context of the schematic shown.

Fire away! Just be fair by remembering, I was only the messenger.

The second important aspect of this book strategy is for the reader to understand how new ideas find their way into the public conscience, which is as follows: It is difficult if not impossible for authors to offer new health-related ideas that have not been subjected to peer review. The escape mechanism for persistent authors is to end up writing a book that can be self-published. The reader can find that many successful authors have taken that path.

Book Structure

Apparently, sustaining an embolic stroke following a thirty-seven-year career with NIH and Pfizer on medically related topics conditions an inquisitive mind to view stroke and heart attack differently from conventional ideas of the diseases. You will find that I have thoroughly endorsed the Einstein quote.

While documenting my stroke experience coupled with intensive literature searches over the past three years, two major departures from usual stroke thinking were developed:

1. A schematic was constructed showing proposed mechanisms explaining how and why blood clots can form in the heart (not relying upon arrhythmia).
   - Why African Americans will have a higher stroke and heart attack risk than Caucasians.
   - Why TIAs[1] may not be recognized as symptoms of both heart attack and stroke.
   - Why TIA effects are of short duration and without residual tissue damage.
2. A unique hypothesis for mechanisms of neuropathy is offered.

Here is a brief outline of how this account will unfold: I am going to try to make a rational case for how a state of dehydration coupled with any of a variety of cofactors could together provide the mechanism for clot formation leading to embolic stroke and/or heart attack. Each of the potential co-factors will be separately discussed, to build a plausible hypothesis of stroke mechanisms if possible. There are, of course, the conventionally recognized stroke risk factors to be considered in any comprehensive account—age, blood pressure, lipid profile, etc.

In addition, here is the outline of hypothesized co-factors to be discussed, along with their supporting literature references.

---

1   TIA: Transient ischemic attack (spelled ischemic in British English (abbreviated as TIA, often colloquially referred to as "mini stroke") is a change in the blood supply.

A) Dehydration
B) Arrhythmia
C) Insulin Resistance
D) Fibrinogen
E) Stress Hormones
F) Red Cell Agglutinating Agents
   1. Influenza Virus
   2. Mycoplasma
   3. Sickle Cell Disease
   4. Rheumatoid Arthritis
   5. Magnesium Deficiency

During the course of my experience with embolic stroke, I formulated these proposed stroke/heart attack mechanisms which seem to lie outside the framework of traditional explanations. Those who are trained in stroke matters may be able to endorse or refute these ideas as subjects of common knowledge, ignorance, or naivety…maybe all of the above. Readers may decide for themselves.

Not having come across anyone who would or could offer counsel, I leave the test of truth to someone else for now and welcome constructive comment. As I get the picture, I think there are several less-traveled streets within Stroke City that need to be remapped and given new signage. These streets are named Dehydration, Arrhythmia, Insulin Resistance, Fibrinogen, and Inflammatory Agents. Each is reviewed as a separate discussion topic. Additional topics covered are:

A) Brief description of how my embolic stroke made its presence known. (See Chapter 2: How the Odyssey Began)
B) Description of the types of strokes that are available, some stroke and heart attack statistics, and the rationale behind the "stroke belt" observed.
C) A review of risk factors that stroke and heart attack have in common.

Main Message of Book

While the original intent of the book was an account of how and why I was affected by an embolic stroke and what the reader can do to minimize his or her stroke risk, it became evident that a much greater purpose could be served by showing how stroke (S) and heart attack (HA) have common roots and common causes.

This book is intended to describe in first person what it is like to experience an embolic stroke, and to distinguish it from other types of stroke. It is meant to be a handbook on what to expect after an embolic stroke. It is a *who, what, why, when, where,* and *how* type of stroke information. It is a guide for available treatment options I have studied, and my assessment of their utility. The book is strongly committed to offering reasons why my stroke (or your stroke) need never have happened.

While my main focus had been on stroke, coming to my senses on March 24, 2010, I realized that what was really going on within my studies was the revelation that a case possibly could be made that both heart attack and stroke, very likely have common root causes.

This book is a product of my research of stroke literature, along with my ideas, revealing what you can do—starting today—to prevent stroke and heart attack. Some are new strategies neither currently recognized/ endorsed, nor refuted by the stroke industry. They simply seem not to have been considered.

STROKE SCIENCE

Types of Stroke

There are five major types of strokes. Two are caused by clots, two by hemorrhage, and one (in theory) by blood vessel spasm (TIA). The two caused by clots, cerebral thrombosis and cerebral embolism, account for 70 to 80 percent of all strokes. Hemorrhagic strokes have a much higher fatality rate than strokes caused by clots (University of Tennessee Medical Center website, *Types of Stroke*). Strokes caused by cerebral and subarachnoid hemorrhages are caused by ruptured blood vessels. In my opinion, warning strokes are probably caused by a blood vessel spasm.

Cerebral thrombosis: Cerebral thrombosis, the most common kind of stroke, occurs when a blood clot forms in an artery, blocking the flow of blood to the brain. A warning stroke (TIA) often precedes these types of strokes.

Cerebral embolism: This type of stroke occurs when a blood clot forms in other parts of the body and is carried to the brain where it blocks blood flow. A heart disorder called atrial fibrillation is said to be a risk factor for this kind of stroke.

Subarachnoid hemorrhage: This type of stroke is caused when a blood vessel on the surface of the brain ruptures, bleeding into the space between the brain and the skull.

Cerebral hemorrhage: About 10 percent of strokes are cerebral hemorrhages, which occur when an artery in the brain bursts because of a head injury or an aneurysm. An aneurysm is a weak blood vessel that swells out like a balloon. Though they're not always dangerous, the artery wall can weaken and burst.

Warning stroke: A stroke without lasting damage because, in theory, it is caused by a spastic blood vessel (usually called a TIA).

Similarities of Stroke and Heart Attack Risk Factors

- Advancing age
- Elevated blood pressure
- Coronary artery disease
- Inactivity
- Obesity
- Diabetes (HA and S are the greatest cause of death among diabetics.)
- Family history
- Stress
- Tobacco
- Blood clots

The crucial fact that emerges from this tabulation is that both of these major killers have the same MO. In both cases, it is a clot that blocks oxygen and nutrients from reaching nerve cells in the brain (stroke) and muscle cells in the heart (heart attack). On the surface, this seems like a pretty simple problem to solve: prevent unwanted clot formation and you prevent HA and S.

Okay, so why have our research centers not been able to solve these problems—given the huge investment in health research made over the years? From my stroke experience, I am going to tell you what I think has been the major mistake and how I think these problems should be approached.

The following pages detail statistical data for heart attack and stroke from the US Centers for Disease Control and Prevention, the American Heart Association, and the World Health Association, respectively.

Statistical Dimensions of Heart Attack and Stroke

From the Center for Disease Control and Prevention 2006
(Prevalence and hospitalizations are computed for 2006 unless otherwise indicated. Mortality data are final for 2005, unless otherwise indicated.)

Estimated Annual Occurrence:

Heart disease: 631,636 cases
Cancer: 559,888
Stroke (cerebrovascular disease): 137,119
Chronic lower respiratory diseases: 124,583
Accidents (unintentional injuries): 121,599
Diabetes: 72,449
Alzheimer's disease: 72,432
Influenza and pneumonia: 56,326
Nephritis, nephrotic syndrome, and nephrosis: 45,344
Septicemia: 34,234
Combination of heart disease and stroke: 768,755

The following statistics are from the US Centers for Disease Control and Prevention and the Heart Disease and Stroke Statistics—2010 Update published by the American Heart Association.

Stroke is the third leading cause of death in the United States. Over 143,579 people die each year from stroke in the United States.

Each year, about 795,000 people suffer a stroke. About 600,000 of these are first attacks and 185,000 are recurrent attacks.

Stroke is the leading cause of serious, long-term disability in the United States.

Nearly three-quarters of all strokes occur in people over the age of sixty-five. The risk of having a stroke more than doubles each decade after the age of fifty-five.

Strokes can—and do—occur at *any* age. Nearly one-quarter of strokes occur in people under the age of sixty-five.

Stroke death rates are higher for African Americans than for Caucasians, even at younger ages.

In 2005, among adults age twenty and older, the number of people who had strokes was 6,500,000 (about 2,600,000 males and 3,900,000 females).

On average, every forty seconds, someone in the United States has a stroke.

Each year, about 55,000 more women than men have a stroke. Men's stroke incidence rates are greater than women's at younger ages but not at older ages. The male/female incidence ratio is 1.25 at ages fifty five to sixty-four; 1.50 for ages sixty-five to seventy-four; 1.07 at seventy-five to eighty-four; and 0.76 at eighty-five and older.

Of all strokes, 87 percent are ischemic, 10 percent are intracerebral hemorrhage, and 3 percent are sub-arachnoid hemorrhage.

Stroke accounted for about one of every seventeen deaths in the United States in 2005. Stroke mortality for 2005 was 143,579 (56,586 males, 86,993 females).

From 1995 to 2005, the stroke death rate fell 29.7 percent and the actual number of stroke deaths declined 13.5 percent.

The risk of ischemic stroke in current smokers is about double that of nonsmokers, after adjustment for other risk factors.

Atrial fibrillation (AF) is an independent risk factor for stroke, increasing risk about five-fold.

High blood pressure is the most important risk factor for stroke.

<u>From the World Health Organization 2007</u>
<u>and the American Heart Association</u>

According to the World Health Organization, 15 million people suffer stroke worldwide each year. Of these, 5 million die and another 5 million are permanently disabled.

High blood pressure contributes to over 12.7 million strokes worldwide.

Europe averages approximately 650,000 stroke deaths each year.

In developed countries, the incidence of stroke is declining—largely due to efforts to lower blood pressure and reduce smoking. However, the overall rate of stroke remains high due to the aging of the population.

Sources: World Health Report—2007, from the World Health Organization; International Cardiovascular Disease Statistics (2007 Update), a publication from the American Heart Association.

The Stroke Belt

If one is looking for more convincing evidence for dehydration contributing to stroke, there is a rather compelling geographic pattern of stroke in America. I am referring to the "stroke belt" that extends through the southeastern states. When you think about this pattern of stroke as possibly related to dehydration, it is easy to justify this clustering of stroke. The fact that those states are characterized as both hot and humid creates the environment for excessive perspiration, and thus increased dehydration potential. Of course, there are other factors that enter the picture, such as higher percentage of African Americans in the general population.

As described in another section of the book, a case is made for higher stroke risk in African Americans, due to their propensity for sickle cell disease, which adds another layer of risk to that population, according to the hypothesis developed around the schematic. Since there does not seem to be any clustering of stroke in hot, dry areas of the United States, one can guess that those living in that area intuitively know they must consume more water, which has become a natural part of their lifestyle.

So there you have it, as I see the picture. Those who live in a hot, humid area will dehydrate more readily than those living in temperate zones, and thus are more vulnerable to stroke.

But wait a minute. If this is true, then we should expect a similar cluster of heart attacks in the stroke belt. Checking into that point of view, I did come across the notation by a public service bulletin by Health Key referring to the CDC Behavioral Risk Factor Surveillance System (BRFSS) stating, "Ongoing (telephone) survey by the Center for Disease Control indicate that people in some regions of the US—particularly the Southeast—have a higher risk of chronic heart disease because of various social and economic factors." This bulletin, as quoted, did not specifically distinguish between stroke and heart attack rates, but the implication is there as a starting place for anyone wishing to pursue more details.

Thus, this book is an effort to document how these diseases are related, both in cause and in prevention. The Chapters refer to the science of stroke and the Lessons refer to the experience of stroke.

Stroke Belt

Here are additional goals:

To show why there is hope to avoid S and HA, even if you have a strong family history of these diseases.

To reveal a hypothesized mechanism schematic for S and HA that will show how and why changing selected aspects of your lifestyle can minimize your risk.

To describe a new way of looking at neuropathy associated with neurologic diseases.

To show why African Americans will have a higher S and HA risk than Caucasians.

To discuss treatment modalities I have evaluated.

A brief on how my embolic stroke unfolded and what you must watch for.

Proposed mechanisms for warning stroke and heart attack.

Who Needs This Book

Foremost, this book was written for every person age fifty and older who has had an embolic stroke (or is vulnerable) who wants to know what to expect from the experience and how to prevent another stroke.

This book is for everyone who takes responsibility for their own health strategy and wants to know what they can do to minimize their heart and stroke risk—starting today.

This book is for vascular research scientists and practitioners who are willing to look at these diseases without the restrictions imposed by historical views of them.

Why I May Be Uniquely Qualified to Write this Account of Stroke

It is well known that stroke is an affliction born mostly by those of us with the most life experience. As a consequence, when trying to sort out which symptoms to target with any treatment strategy, one is confronted with the question as to whether the issue is stroke or simply age-related. This is a very real consideration since on more than one occasion, I have had medical professionals remind me that I am growing older and that my stroke issue also is consistent with the aging process; both observations are hard to dispute. For me, we are talking the late seventies at that point. Also, it can be a bit embarrassing to ask your doctor for a remedy for old age.

As an 81-year old with a scientific background and given that advancing age is considered a risk factor for stroke, I may be the only person to have recorded firsthand stroke effects when combined with advanced age. This combination was made possible by the fact that I have spent a lifetime in medically related research.

While I am not a clinician, neither do most clinicians have firsthand knowledge of the stroke experience; thus, we both can provide useful perspectives.

CHAPTER TWO

How The Odyssey Began

To Educate or Impress—Which Is Our Goal?

When we start talking about stroke, we really need to begin with an understanding of what drives the way we talk. It is notable that not only the physicians but also the medical press seem to intentionally use technical medical jargon to confuse the public. As for stroke, a case in point is the term "TIA", which is an acronym for transient ischemic attack. Most folks cannot decide even how to pronounce the word. Is it IS-KEEMIC or ISH-EEMIC? So why not agree there are just two fundamental types of stroke: one is a warning stroke (now called a TIA) and the other is a for-real stroke. The former is what the medical profession and press use to impress; it's certainly not to inform. What should be done is to state the event in understandable and meaningful language that a TIA is, in fact, a warning stroke. We should acknowledge both that it is a stroke and that it immediately should be managed as one. If we can change that mindset, then there will be less likelihood the event will be dismissed when the symptoms go away in a matter of hours or days. Here is another term that needs to be eliminated: *idiopathic,* which is a fancy medical designation for "we have no clue what is causing the problem." Along that same line, we are often told that "we don't know the *exact* cause of death." This implies that we know what caused death, all except for some very fine biochemical detail. Why not just tell the truth? "We have no idea why the patient died—the missing exact biochemical detail (if there ever was one) is of no importance anyway; dead is dead."

From my experience, I can tell you with confidence that you must be vigilant to know you have even experienced a warning stroke. I thought my first warning stroke was so unusual that while later suspected, I certainly did not know what really happened until several years later when an MRI film (scan of my brain) following my first recognized TIA was read and they spotted an old brain lesion. It played out like this: I was driving between Terre Haute and Indianapolis, Indiana, when my left arm suddenly felt like it was floating in air. The sensation disappeared within an hour, as did my concern for the event, but wonder of its significance always remained in the back of my mind.

Stroke Event History

My first recognized warning stroke event occurred at eleven AM, May 21, 2005, while living in Florida. I was mowing grass in Florida several years after my unrecognized event happened in Indiana. In this case I knew immediately what was going on and went to an emergency room. The effects lasted seventy two hours and disappeared with no residual signs—not unusual for a warning stroke (TIA). There were no residual effects after a few hours, so I am beginning to get the hang of this routine: wait long enough and you will be just fine. The problem is that you cannot know if you are experiencing a warning or a real stroke. YOU MUST ASSUME IT IS A REAL STROKE TO HAVE ANY CHANCE FOR INTERVENTION. YOU MUST GET YOURSELF TO AN ER, HOPEFULLY WITHIN A STROKE CENTER.

My third recognized warning stroke occurred a few weeks after the second and was a case where my knees buckled as I stood up on the morning of June 11, 2005.

The real stroke event that led to my lasting physical damage occurred August 24, 2007, was actually recognized by my wife while I was reading the morning paper. She entered the room and noticed I was tipped toward one side of the chair, holding the paper cockeyed. I showed facial contortion and was drooling—of which I was totally unaware. This event occurred after my primary care physician failed to insist that I not discontinue taking the blood-thinning drug Coumadin after I related to him how much I disliked taking it because I had observed spots on my skin where blood seemed evident beneath the surface. I said to him, "If Coumadin is doing this to my skin, what the world might it be doing to other organs in my body?" He must have been persuaded by my point because he said, "I don't blame you. If I had the problem, I would not use it either." Net result: six weeks after stopping the drug, I had a full-blown stroke. Parenthetically, I had forgotten that when I previously used this same argument with my Florida doc, he wisely said, "You cannot stop taking the drug; you have had a stroke". By the way, relating this story to yet another doctor, he dismissed the idea of bleeding under the skin as related to Coumadin. Hard to know what or who to believe sometimes—as you too will probably discover eventually.

Here is part of the problem: If you have a skilled primary care physician for your warning stroke (TIA) as I had in Florida, the doctor (KT) will insist that you take a blood thinner. At the time of this writing, the blood thinner of choice is usually Coumadin (Warfarin). When you start looking into the history of that drug, you will learn that it was first used as a rat poison. That image tends to dominate the thought process, making the notion of using the drug thoroughly repulsive. But what is missing in this equation is that for stroke-prevention purposes, the stuff usually works and will provide needed protection from unwanted clot formation, which can lead from a warning (TIA) to a stroke. To get through this process, my advice is to get over the idea you are having to take a rat poison—and be damned glad there is an agent proven to be safe and usually effective when used and monitored correctly. By monitored, I mean that you will become familiar with the terms pro time[1] and INR,[2] as these are tests you must have done on a regular basis to be sure the level of Coumadin is proper. Diet, drugs, and nutrients

---

1   Pro Time: Prothrombin time (PT) is a blood test that measures how long it takes blood to clot. A prothrombin time test can be used to check for bleeding problems. PT is also used to check whether medicine to prevent blood clots is working.
2   INR: International Normalized Ratio: The prothrombin time (PT) and its derived measures of prothrombin ratio (PR) and international normalized ratio (INR) are measures of the extrinsic pathway of coagulation.

also can affect blood clotting and upset your dosage regimen—so be prepared for that experience as well. Generally speaking, you will have your pro time or INR checked on a daily to weekly basis when first starting out using this drug, and then, with experience, your doctors may find when your INR pattern is sufficiently stable so that they can recommend a safe testing interval, perhaps as long as five or six weeks. In any event, this is the one wrinkle you just have to endure.

Here is a stroke hint for you: **Do not wait for three warning strokes to occur before getting it through your head that you need fast and continuous medical supervision to prevent a real stroke.** This single bit of advice will more than pay for the cost of your kids' college education.

But don't forget: my hidden agenda is to get stroke facts and new ideas to you by any truthful and understandable means I can devise.

If the stroke industry must have an acronym to accomplish its educational goal, I suggest we simply refer to a warning stroke as a Big Deal. In fact, to be politically correct and a little more colorful, we could call it a BFD. If we agree that this is appropriately descriptive, then this demands that Vice President Joe Biden be recognized as the first courageous soul to earn an honorary medical degree for his perceptive description of a warning stroke—as that acronym really does reflect the scene perfectly.

Character Builders

One of the features of my generation was the notion that if you wanted to go to college, you paid for it yourself, and that's exactly what I did for all eight years. I paid for it by working as many jobs as I could find. For example, the summer before I started grad school in Ann Arbor, I had three jobs. In the morning, I worked for the City of Alma, digging graves. In the afternoon, I drove a busload of kids to Rock Lake to swim. In the evening, I worked in a gas station. On one occasion, at age eighteen or nineteen, while driving home from the lake (probably twelve to fifteen miles), the brakes on the bus went out—totally gone. What to do? Load of kids, no brakes, no phone. Well, I drove the distance in lowest gear, up and down modest hills at the slowest pace possible, crossing railroad tracks on two occasions, but finally getting back to bus garage safely. Whew!

As for grave-digging, I can tell you they were not the traditional six feet deep; they were one shovel length deep—and if in clay, probably even less. While working at the gas station, an older gentleman named Volney Church said to me, "Oh, I remember you: You are the one I picked up off the highway in front of the gas station after you fell out of your dad's nine-passenger car." Yes indeed, that was me. In a big family, you can fall out of car and not be missed. As it turned out, I fell out a second time a few minutes later. I must say while working at the gas station, I was not an innocent player as Volney, whose teeth were worn down where his pipe was positioned, left his pipe on the bench where we repaired inner tubes. There was always a pile of rubber dust where we abraded the inner tubes before patching. I spotted this and packed his pipe with rubber dust, and then overlaid it with tobacco so it would be ready to go for his next smoke—a fine way to treat a guy who probably saved my life. Sorry, Volney, but it seemed funny at the time, and I knew you could not catch me.

For character building, you really need to know about my mother, Eleanor. Picture this: In 1935, at the start of the Great Depression, I was six years old when my father died. Mother had no source of income, eleven children, and a fierce determination not to go on welfare. Although she had no college experience, she surely could have been a full professor in the School of Common Sense, with a minor in Spare the Rod. My younger brother, Lynn, and I finally hid the razor strap. She passed the exam to qualify as a social worker for the state of Michigan and thus provide essentials for her large family. It turned out, even as poor as we were, Mother was always making clothing and providing food for some of her clients, who were even worse off than we were.

Growing up, we learned the fine art of how to trace our foot pattern on a piece of cardboard and then cut it out to make inserts for our shoes, keeping snow from direct contact with our feet. Here are a couple of character memories: The most dreaded days in grade school were when we had to remove our shoes to be weighed. The trick was to walk past all the other kids while shuffling your feet along, so as not to reveal that the hand-me-down stockings had no toes. Then there was the unforgettable time a teacher asked us what we had for breakfast. When I said that we had eaten oatmeal, she replied, "Oats! That is what you feed horses." You can imagine the embarrassment this hungry child felt. We occasionally did get a half pint of milk that was in excess of what other kids had paid to receive. To this day, I still like the taste of room-temperature milk. This was at a time when skim milk, usually dumped in the sewer by the Alma Dairy, was sold for ten cents a gallon.

Character building? Here is another one. During high school days, I never studied (as my grades would testify). Nevertheless, I was accepted at Alma College, where I paid $300 per semester for tuition while living at home. In my first semester, I took chemistry, physics, German, English, and orientation. At the end of my first semester, I had passed English and orientation—and had failed chemistry, physics, and German. But you know what? I always viewed this as the best thing that ever happened to me. For the first time, I began the process of learning how to study and then applying myself. I was able to graduate in four years (although I was on academic probation most of that time).

Life Experiences Along the Way

Here is an example of getting humble in a hurry. While earning money for college, I worked at the Alma Piston Company. The plant manager, Mr. Davies, was a most considerate gentleman, knowing my intention to go to grad school at U of M, he allowed me to work overtime and put me in charge of the first-aid station.

One of my buddies, Pete Sanford, kept pestering me to lance a boil on his thigh above his knee. I reminded him that must be done by a doctor, but he persisted until I relented. So I sat him down in front of me on a stool, painted the area with tincture of iodine, sterilized a needle, and stuck it into the center. I was hunched over the site and gently pressed on each side of the boil. Wrong thing to do! In an instant, what did not hit me square in the face hit the ceiling of the room. If this was not enough, I said, "Pete, let's see if we got all of this", so I repeated the routine, and this time what blood did not hit me, hit the ceiling.

Talk about a slow learner. Pete had an uneventful recovery, and I got a grin and a thank you. We both had a good laugh.

While working at NIH, I was in charge of glassware and the tissue culture prep lab (low man on totem pole syndrome). I had one fellow who always came to work drunk. I said to Sam (not his name), "You know Sam, if you can't come to work sober, I am going to have to let you go". He was a tall guy with odor of alcohol surrounding him, and with his blood shot eyes and a slur, he said to me, "Jeeze Chriz Doc, I have done everything I can think of to get over this problem; why I even joined Alcoholics Unanimous".

I think about how I got accepted for grad school at University of Michigan as a candidate who did not have anything going in terms of academic excellence – here is how it unfolded, and you can decide. I am interviewed on a Friday afternoon by the Chairman of the Department of Microbiology, whose name was Dr. Harvey Soule. There was nothing remarkable about my interview that I could recognize, and yet there was something very remarkable going on I did not realize until I returned to my home in Alma and read headlines in the newspaper the next day, that "Dr. Harvey Soule famous U of M scientist, took his life by injecting himself with snake venom." I could look at it this way; had I been the subject of a committee decision; it is very likely I would not have been accepted. This thought (60 years after the fact) did not occur to me until writing this manuscript, but viewed in terms of synchronicity, it is quite possible that our lives were entwined so that my life could unfold as it was supposed to – expressed more eloquently by others—it is my view that nothing happens by chance, there are no accidents, we live in a perfect universe.

Dr. Soule must have seen something in me that lead him to think I was a reasonable gamble, possibly comforted by knowing at the time that he was out of here, and I would not be his problem. I was without doubt, his final student admitted to U of M. I do wish I knew what convinced him. I thought he seemed like a really nice guy. Of course he might have thought, "So this is what the world is coming to." Lordy.

To get through grad school, one must maintain a B average or better while taking some classes with med students so considering my rocky start, this was quite an accomplishment. Maybe he was impressed by my tenacity, which has been characterized as "like a sand burr buried in dog's hair".

CHAPTER THREE

Proposed Stroke And Heart Attack Mechanisms

Introduction

There are two hypothesized stroke mechanisms at work beneath all others. The first is a mechanism to account for warning strokes and warning heart attacks (TIAs). This mechanism involves the formation of spastic blood vessels, which temporarily shuts off blood supply to a small portion of the brain or heart. This version of the mechanics accounts for the temporary effect of a TIA, since the vessel will relax rather quickly, allowing blood supply to resume.

The second mechanism, involving permanent tissue damage, is where a blood clot migrates to a site in the brain or heart, blocking blood flow. This leads to more permanent damage because the clot is not dissolved fast enough to allow blood return to the tissue.

In the schematic shown for this theory, you will find that behind both warning and real events that coupled with dehydration lays a magnesium deficiency and/or an excess of a stress hormone such as cortisol.

These circumstances can cause both a blood vessel spasm (TIA) associated with temporary stroke damage, or can cause sticky cells that lead to clot formation associated with permanent damage. Thus whether our bodies are faced with a warning or a real event, they share identical etiologic agents. Confirming studies would be required and welcomed.

What this is really saying is that the machinery is in place for another, and perhaps more serious event, so take heed.

What I draw from this idea is that these vascular events can be either a one- or a two-step process. It is one step if the first HA or S is not preceded by the body having signaled a warning, which can be in the form of a TIA (transient ischemic attack) involving either the heart or the brain. Without the warning TIA, then the body sees only a full-blown S or HA. In this case, a blood clot blocks oxygen and nutrients from entering nerve or muscle tissue. A heart attack or stroke lies ahead, and the severity will depend upon how much of the organ is deprived. I believe the root mechanism for this type of problem is very likely within the schematic options shown with dehydration, magnesium deficiency, and/or cortisol as major players.

In the two-step sequence, a totally different mechanism is predicted. In this case, a warning is given by the body, appearing as a TIA, which can manifest either in the heart or the brain. The projected mechanism this time involves a spasm of a blood vessel which shuts down the blood supply to a small portion of the heart or brain and is of short duration, since blood flow is restored with relaxation of the spasm but gives the appearance of a stroke or heart attack. This does, of course, offer an explanation as to why we can quickly recover from a mini-stroke or mini HA without after-effects, while with a full-blown S or HA, we are left with permanent damage. Interestingly, both the TIA spasm as well as a full S or HA also can be the products of a magnesium deficiency, but probably is coupled with elevated stress hormone, as both can cause vessel spasms.

It All Seems so Clear to Me Now

There is a term called synchronicity, defined as a "happen chance" which occurs, that is in perfect alignment with your thoughts or ideas. This means, to me at least, that whatever information you need to accomplish your goals will surface exactly when you need it. Examples of synchronicity occurred so many times during preparation of this manuscript that I have lost count. But let me give you a recent example of what I mean.

On several occasions in the last few years, my wife Sylvia has experienced what could be called false heart attacks (FHA) with the "elephant on her chest" and squeezing sensation occurring and disappearing after deep breathing. She, of course, went through the usual catalogue of heart tests, where the cardiologists could find nothing to account for her symptoms. Her blood pressure is always in the low range, and those events—while never associated with activity— certainly could be equated with stressful events. After her most recent experience (August 14, 2010), I of course suggested again she see a doctor, and as usual, she rejected that idea, having experienced it so many times before. This put me on the path to restudy her problem with maximum persistence. I reasoned that perhaps her symptoms were the result of a coronary blood vessel going into a spasm, temporarily blocking blood supply to the heart muscle, leading to a sort of a TIA or warning heart attack. This idea seemed entirely reasonable, since her symptoms were never associated with physical activity and were short-lived. Thus, I did an Internet study to see if cortisol (a stress hormone) had been associated with heart attack symptoms. Indeed, there are numerous reports where spasms of heart blood vessels could simulate heart attack symptoms. Knowing that blood vessel constriction is also associated with magnesium deficiency, as noted in Appendix VI, we immediately started a magnesium addition to her diet. Only time will tell if that will help prevent future episodes. But here is where synchronicity enters the picture.

The following morning, as I was passing through the kitchen where she was preparing breakfast, I stopped abruptly in my tracks, and said, "Oh my gosh—what you have experienced is *exactly* what I have been going through for several years. It is just that your symptoms refer to your heart, while mine referred to my brain." That stunning flash immediately seemed to connect the dots, allowing me to predict that her version of a spasm would manifest as an FHA, while mine would manifest as a warning stroke. But it seemed to me that the underlying mechanism for cause and control in both cases is possibly identical: a likely magnesium deficiency, perhaps coupled with cortisol. If the predicted magnesium deficiency and cortisol are not corrected, then a future heart attack for her or another stroke for me would be inevitable.

These pathways to stroke and heart attack are what I have come to believe are at the root of these two major killers, and as discussed later, that very possibly, dehydration also has connections with cancer and to Alzheimer's as well.

Schematic Introduction

The subject of the first half of the book is crystallized and condensed into the following schematic/flowchart.

There are four pillars supporting the structure, which include: dehydration, arrhythmia, red cell clumping agents, and insulin resistance. The general pattern of stroke and heart attack development is shown as the convergence of several possible co-factors that produce a sticky-cell stage which is followed by clot formation. Those events are then followed by the ultimate catastrophes of heart attack or stroke.

SCHEMATIC FOR PROPOSED
STROKE/HEART ATTACK MECHANISMS

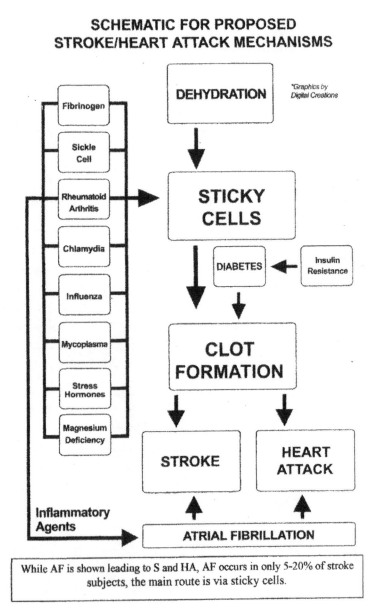

Schematic

Schematic Interpretation

Following dehydration, the next major step in the proposed mechanism for stroke (S) and heart attack (HA), is the sticky-cell stage or phase.

Sticky cells are pictured as the necessary preconditioning step for red cells and platelets that enable them to clot readily. This is a more formalized idea of why clots form during the course of S and HA development, which does not rely on atrial fibrillation to provide a likely mechanism. Naturally, formation of clot serves as the final villain for S and HA etiology.

Backing up for a moment, shown on the left side of the schematic are eight potential co-factors that can couple with dehydration to produce sticky cells.

Here is the big Kahuna that welds this schematic into a coherent pattern: each of the eight co-factors shown on the left side of the schematic, from fibrinogen through magnesium deficiency, is by itself capable of inducing or promoting atrial fibrillation.

The vehicle that ties them together is inflammation. AF seems to get a lot of credit for S and HA; it should be clear according to this proposed flow chart that actually AF per se is only a matter of guilt by association. Beneath AF is an entire complex of inflammatory agents which alone or in concert are at the true roots of HA and S.

You will notice too, the prominent role of insulin resistance and subsequent diabetes that are shown as a means by which the sticky-cell stage can be bypassed. Since diabetes and its associated metabolic syndrome components are capable of inducing clot formation directly, I think it is fair to speculate that the one thing AF does bring to the table is to provide a theoretical mechanical means to reduce clot size to a range that can block small vessels, allowing them to migrate either to the heart for HA or to the brain for S.

According to the University of Maryland Heart Center, AF is associated with stroke risk at a rate of 5 percent and is responsible for 70,000 to 100,000 strokes a year. According to CDC, 2.6 million will have AF in 2010, with AF responsible for 15 to 20 percent of strokes, which conflicts with the Maryland data. Five percent of 2.6 million previously quoted would amount to 130,000 strokes, so those numbers are in range. Saying this in another way, as I interpret the data, 95 percent of subjects with AF have no increased stroke risk, so AF per se is not the target.

They go on to note that the Warfarin blood thinner reduces stroke by 60 to 70 percent but does not eliminate risk as I can testify.

When we speak of our bodies as being dehydrated, we simply mean that our bodies are producing more fluid as waste than we are drinking—not a safe arrangement. Fibrinogen does not itself cause or prevent a stroke but can help cause the conditions where a stroke or heart attack can occur. Fibrinogen is a crucial chemical called a proenzyme in our blood that helps stop bleeding after injury—but too much can be harmful, causing clots to form when we do not need them. In fact, you could think of magnesium deficiency, chlamydia, influenza, and mycoplasma infections as well as sickle cell and rheumatoid arthritis diseases as having the common behavior, in that they do not themselves cause stroke or heart attack but increase risk by providing the conditions for clots to form that lead to stroke and heart attack. Diabetes seems to be the exception by directly causing clot formation, creating an even higher risk of stroke.

Diabetes is an epidemic disease in which, because of the lack of a particular hormone, sugar can accumulate in the blood, instead of being changed into energy or fat. **High sugar in our blood** can cause blood to clot. The clots apparently can be broken up into smaller clots by a rapidly beating heart (atrial fibrillation). The small clots then can travel into tiny blood vessels in the brain or heart muscles, clogging them such that neither oxygen nor food can reach the cells, causing them to die, which is then is termed a stroke or heart attack.

The reason for this discussion is to offer a possible mechanism for clot formation in AF events that does not rely solely on an erratic heartbeat and thus may offer a possible explanation why not all AF events lead to heart attack or stroke. Doctors and patients need to understand this difference so that they can make appropriate changes in their health habits to help avoid these two diseases. From this discussion, it should be evident that the most important changes we can make are to drink much more water and to be sure we have good nutrition that includes a rich magnesium supply. The current recommended amount is eight glasses of water per day. It is highly unlikely that clots are caused by a deficiency of a prescription drug such as Plavix or the like.

A Fly in the Ointment

The notion that blood clots are at the root of heart attack and stroke seems pretty clear and reasonable. What is not obvious is that according to my schematic, there are several ways red cells can clump together to form a clot-like blocking agent, fully capable of interfering with blood flow in the heart or brain.

Red cells are not involved with clot formation, thus a blood thinning agent such as Coumadin is not going to be able to prevent all forms of blockage, and therefore cannot be 100% effective in preventing future HA or S as is recognized. My own experience testifies to that point. My blood chemistry profile showed that my clotting index was indeed at the desired level (2.5) when my second warning stroke (TIA) occurred. At the time, I thought this could be explained by the idea that a warning stroke is a product of a blood vessel spasm rather than a clot (my theory). The upshot of this picture is that into the mix of risk factors that can contribute to S or HA, the addition of the red cell clumping agents shown in the schematic must now be considered. This theoretical dimension of S and HA offers a new target for the management of these diseases. Unfortunately, I have no suggestions as to how to prevent sickled cells or virus-infected cells from forming lethal associations, as that is a mission for our vascular research centers.

DISCUSSION TOPICS

Arrhythmia

With the close association of arrhythmia as a stated risk factor for stroke, I reviewed the literature for evidence of its possible impact on my stroke. To do that, it was necessary to retrace some medical history. Following a consultation with a cardiologist in Terre Haute, Indiana, in 2004 for arrhythmia management, I was introduced to the drug Mexelitine, which I used for several months with good control of symptoms. During my hospital stay (which was required while introducing that drug), I suggested to an associate of my doctor covering for the weekend that my symptoms seemed consistent with stress/anxiety. He agreed and gave me Alprazolam (Xanax), which quite remarkably was associated with an immediate drop in blood pressure and disappearance of arrhythmia. This was a turning point in my view of my health management, since I came to believe any solution must include stress control. However, I did not want to have to rely on Xanax either. Having read all I could find on the problem, I came to believe that a beta blocker might control the problem. Since I had tried Atenolol previously (and found that this drug seemed to exacerbate my arrhythmia), I asked if I could try a beta blocker again but at a lower dose. Why I thought a beta blocker might be more desirable than Xanax, I have no idea. The doctor prescribed Toprol XL along with Norvasc, which successfully controlled pressure and arrhythmia very well for two years. However, in early 2006, my mild arrhythmia returned. After an in-depth search of medically-related literature, I found references to the successful use of potassium, calcium, magnesium combination, plus flax oil to manage irregular heartbeat. With the addition of those items to my diet, I got along very well until November of 2006, when I again experienced arrhythmia. Based on earlier experience, I took a tablet of Alprazolam, which restored normal rhythm. I thus launched another investigation, and this is where it got interesting.

I found numerous references where sawdust was associated with arrhythmia. Most of the reports were extracted from Material Safety

Data sheets where OSHA[1] monitors health issues among workers. During the previous two weeks before this outbreak of arrhythmia, I had been sawing and turning cherry wood, making a cradle. I found references to sawdust acting as an allergen,[2] which then led me to look into histamine[3] in terms of arrhythmia, since that agent is closely allied with allergic reactions. Investigating the role of histamine in arrhythmia, I found a rich history of histamine-induced/associated arrhythmia. Investigating the role of histamines as related to stress/anxiety, I also found significant evidence of arrhythmia associated with stress/anxiety. With the pieces of this puzzle seeming to come together, I needed to find out how or why Alprazolam fit into the picture. Surprisingly to me, I found out that Alprazolam is a known antihistamine, a fact that seems to tie pieces of this odyssey together. As a final notation, I found where cherry wood is one of several recognized wood allergens.

In a continuation of this study, I began a review of the role of histamine in a variety of disease processes. They are numerous and lie outside the scope of this book. I did find that some antihistamines are very proarrhythmic[4] and could be counter-productive or dangerous for arrhythmia management.

At least in my case, there seemed to be the suggestion of possibly three targets for management of my arrhythmia; there seemed to be a stress/anxiety component, an allergic component, which in either case seemed to be eased with Alprazolam, and then apparently a magnesium/flax oil component for sticky-cell management.

As a further notation: Even in the face of the above discussion, I later experienced scattered events of arrhythmia during night or day. I then reminded myself of the importance of flax oil, and the calcium, potassium, and magnesium caplets. I realized I had become very cavalier in their use, sometimes skipping a few days at a time. As another gut check, in November of 2006, I awoke with a significant arrhythmia

1   OSHA: Occupational Safety and Health Administration, a government agency in the Department of Labor to maintain a safe and healthy work environment.
2   Allergen: A substance, such as pollen, that causes an allergy.
3   Histamine: Histamine is an organic nitrogen compound involved in local immune responses as well as regulating physiological function in the gut and acting as a neurotransmitter.
4   Proarrhythmic: A chemical, drug, or food that promotes cardiac arrhythmias.

and then realized I again did lathe work the previous evening without adequate protection.

Here is a really interesting part: it was curious that there seemed to be two different patterns to the arrhythmia. There was the usual skipped-beat type, which was usually the predominant pattern, and then a second superimposed pattern where the pulse in the carotid arteries seemed to beat in half step with wrist pulse and this pattern was clearly associated with dust particles (allergic). I can tell you, this dual-beat pattern will get your attention. The unanswered question is then, "What is the relationship of the possible types of arrhythmia to stroke-precipitating events?" I leave that to someone a lot smarter than me. I do offer some suggestions later in the book.

Possible Causes of Arrhythmia

While on this topic, a summary of possible causes of arrhythmia may be helpful, that anyone can find by Googling "Arrhythmia causes". My search revealed the following:

1. Electrical signals in the heart that control beat are delayed or blocked. (I ask, "How and why?")
2. Another part of the heart starts producing electrical signals disrupting the normal heartbeat. (How, why?)
3. Smoking or heavy use of alcohol cocaine, amphetamines, some prescription and OTC[5] drugs, as well as excess caffeine or nicotine (not me).
4. Strong emotional stress sufficient to raise BP and release stress hormones such as cortisol (very understandable).
5. High blood pressure, coronary artery disease, heart failure, and thyroid hormones out of balance can each contribute to arrhythmia.
6. Congenital defect such as Wolff-Parkinson White Syndrome.[6]

---

5 OTC: over-the-counter drugs.
6 Wolff-Parkinson White Syndrome: Wolff-Parkinson-White Syndrome is a condition characterized by abnormal electrical pathways in the heart that cause a disruption of the heart's normal rhythm (arrhythmia).

Another Way to Look at AF (Atrial Fibrillation)

They quiver, they shiver, but they can't get the beat, so AF just continues to peat and repeat.

Actually AF is recognized with four different patterns (Borczuk 2009) which are:

1. Paroxysmal AF—can last up to seven days, but ends spontaneously.
2. Persistent AF—lasts more than seven days and requires chemical or electrical intervention to terminate.
3. Permanent AF—continuous AF that has failed attempts to control.
4. Lone AF—term used to describe AF subjects without structural, cardiac, or pulmonary disease. This group has low risk for clot formation.

AF as seen clinically, there is:

1. AF with structurally normal heart.
2. AF associated with cardiovascular disease.
3. AF with predisposing illnesses such as hypothermia, hyperthyroidism, or as post-operative subjects.

The proportion of strokes associated with chronic AF number 14.7 percent (Wolf et al., 1991). Stated another way, approximately 85 to 95 percent of embolic strokes have no relationship with AF. There are currently 2.3 million subjects affected in the United States (Borczuk).

A Stroke Risk Measure

According to a popular measure for AF-related stroke risk (Gage et al., 2001) called CHADS, (Congestive heart failure, age, diabetes, and stroke) came the following statistics:

For every one hundred patients with an AF CHADS score of 0, about two subjects per year will have a stroke. For every one hundred subjects with a maximum CHADS score of 6, then eighteen subjects per year will have a stroke. For every one hundred subjects with no AF, one per year will have a stroke.

According to the University of Maryland Heart Center, AF is associated with stroke risk at a rate of 5 percent and is responsible for 70,000 to 100,000 strokes per year. Five percent of the 2.3 million would amount to 115,000 strokes, so those numbers are consistent. Saying this in another way, as I interpret their data, 85 to 95 percent of subjects with AF have no increased stroke risk as previously mentioned. They go on to note that Warfarin blood thinner reduces stroke by 60 to 70 percent but does not eliminate risk, as I can testify. According to the CDC, 2.6 million people will have AF in 2010, with AF responsible for 15 to 20 percent of strokes.

The point of this discussion is in defense of the schematic presented, where I show AF as a dead end with no persuasive mechanism by itself for clot formation. The implication is that there must be these or other co-factors to be considered for the mechanism of AF clot formation to remain unchallenged.

When a lay person has to find his own solution to a health problem, the medical schools have either not prepared the student adequately or the answer simply has not been considered. I have noticed this mostly when one enters the world of specialists. It seems that once one is identified as a specialist in any field, the specialist is unlikely to consider a diagnosis that lies outside of the contents of their specialized medical satchel. For example, early in my experience, when trying to get a handle on my arrhythmia, I actually found in my cardiologist's report two very significant (yet seemingly insignificant to my physician) words: "quite anxious". There it was—in black and white—yet absolutely nothing was suggested at that time to test his own observation - !

No bell rang to suggest the possibility that my problem might in fact be stress-related? Nope. How simple might my path have been if, rather than having gone through endless tests that defined the cardiologist's special training, I had been seen as a stress candidate? Instead, I was obviously viewed as a subject who could afford an invasive and expensive procedure.

On one occasion, I had the best-known heart surgeon in Indiana recommend a stent be placed in a heart artery, but then went on to say he could not certify that the stent would solve my arrhythmia issue. When I said to him, "Why then would I want to have a stent procedure?"

Hang on to your hat now, he told me, "Because I have it scheduled".

Neither my wife nor I could believe what we were hearing. We politely declined his suggestion.

I do not mean to paint all specialists with the same brush, as certainly some have been thoughtful and helpful. However, I get the sense that if you have good insurance coverage and a body that likely can handle the procedure, anything can happen. I also believe that damned few people would ever consider challenging their doctor. I feel certain that most folks simply go along with the conundrum that "Doctor knows best." If I had also accepted that path, I would have had a heart bypass five or six years ago—and a stent as well. And here I am, still kicking eight years later—without their recommended invasive heart procedures.

Arrhythmia, although considered a stroke risk factor, clearly requires more depth of study since, as discussed later, A-fib says nothing about how or why clots form in the first place. Like it or not, without that clearly evident, in my opinion, there can be no meaningful progress made to solve two of the major killers, heart attack and stroke. Contributing to improved understanding is the work of Squizzato et al. (2005), where they point out in their conclusions, "Hyperthyroidism is associated with atrial fibrillation and cardioembolic stroke.[7] Hypothyroidism is associated with a worse cardiovascular risk factor profile and leads to progression of atherosclerosis."[8]

---

7   Cardioembolic stroke: The traditional definition of stroke, devised by the World Health Organization in the 1970s, is a "neurological deficit of cerebrovascular cause that persists beyond 24 hours".

8   Atherosclerosis: A specific type of *arteriosclerosis;* the terms are sometimes used interchangeably. Atherosclerosis refers to the buildup of fats in and on the artery walls (plaques), which can restrict blood flow. These plaques can also burst, causing a blood clot. Although atherosclerosis is often considered a heart problem, it can affect arteries anywhere in the body. Atherosclerosis is a preventable and treatable condition.

The real issue surrounding arrhythmia (or AF) as a stroke risk factor is to identify the causes for clot formation in the atria (upper chambers of the heart) in the first place. "Oops! My heart just skipped a beat!" That is what arrhythmia feels like the first time it happens. It gets serious when the heart skips a whole bunch of times, or maybe gets even worse by acting like the brakes failed on a Mack truck with the engine still running full throttle. If this happens, it is called A-fib, which is a signal to get to an emergency room—it can be fatal.

Arrhythmia and Atrial Fibrillation as Related to Stroke

Arrhythmia (A) and its more virulent form, atrial fibrillation (AF), have some common features. Both are forms of an irregular heartbeat mediated by magnesium deficiency, as well as by stress hormones and histamine. I am hypothesizing that in contrast to the usual thinking (where AF is considered a stroke risk factor where blood is said to pool in the heart, allowing it to form clots), the real mechanism for clot formation is a product of any of several agents that have the capacity to precondition red cells shown in the schematic. This feature preconditions red cells, giving them the property of sticky cells. The sticky cells then are the true precursors for a rational clot mechanism that does not rely upon the ill-defined pooling of blood to account for clot formation leading to stroke and heart attack.

Looking ahead, in the second part of the book are the lessons I learned from my embolic stroke experience. These lessons are designed to help educate embolic stroke victims, as well as prepare potential stroke victims for what to expect along that path. Also considered in part two are descriptions of the treatment modalities that I evaluated for purposes of this book. You will also find useful tips on disease management and what post-stroke life is like. Stroke prevention is my most urgent message found herein. Atrial fibrillation in the schematic is shown as contributing to stroke by appearance only—guilt by association.

Dehydration

Dehydration is the first element of the stroke story; here is how it was found. I had a hard time accepting the common explanation that embolic stroke was a product of a blood clot arising from an unstable heartbeat (A-Fib). Until a reasonable mechanism for clot formation was uncovered, I found no incentive to continue either my investigation of stroke or the recording of my personal experience.

Interestingly, in the middle of this dilemma, I came across a book by Batmanghelidj (2003), an Iranian physician who was able to make surprising observations while a political prisoner in Iran tending fellow inmates without the help of medicine. Publication of his book, *You're Not Sick, You're Thirsty,* changed everything for the purpose of my studies. Stroke and seventeen other maladies were catalogued as having dehydration as a common cause. Following this clue, I immediately wanted to find out if dehydration could play into the missing mechanism for clot formation in the vascular system as related to stroke and heart attack. I have summarized my thoughts and findings, which represent an amalgamation of medical studies extracted from numerous sources that suggest there may be a notable relationship between possible changes in blood chemistry associated with dehydration, as well as other medical factors that could promote clot formation, and stroke/heart attack risk—all fashioned into a schematic. (See the flowchart)

This path of reasoning led me to conclude and predict that dehydration eventually will be identified as a major stroke risk factor once appropriate studies are sponsored by NINDS.[9] It is obvious that we need not look to the pharmaceutical industry to produce a study for such a non-prescription remedy. Dehydration, while not currently recognized as a stroke risk factor, merits serious consideration when one becomes aware of the story presented herein. However, there is no gold standard to reliably measure dehydration, so we are left mostly with the perceptive work of Batmanghelidj.

As general support for the role of dehydration in stroke, the report of Berginer, Goldsmith, et al. (1989) is informative. They point out that in an arid climate, the average daily incidence of stroke in the Negev

9   NINDS: National Institute of Neurological Disorders and Stroke.

Desert area was about twice as great on relatively warm days as on relatively cold ones, implying loss of body fluid.

Picking up on Batmanghelidj's clinical experience, it appears that as we age, along with increased stroke risk, the thirst signal diminishes, noted by Kenney and Chiu (2001). Also, it is commonly observed that dehydration is manifested by frequent constipation in elderly and the sedentary.

Looking at stroke with a different lens, I see suggestive evidence that dehydration, as shown in the schematic, may be a rather obvious co-factor for clot formation that only very few authors quote. This is evidence that may fall into the anecdotal category, because there seems to be no record of double-blind investigations (that I could find), and thus, is not mainstream thinking. This face of stroke is seldom mentioned and therefore is essentially undocumented. Dehydration is so basic and unyielding to pharmaceutical remedy and so non-esoteric, it has no significant catalogue of published believers. I am sufficiently convinced intuitively that this is a major stroke risk factor. I have included it as a stroke subject to summarize what I could find for readers who tend to take responsibility for their own health and are willing to ignore the apparent lack of formal proof. The need to recognize dehydration is strengthened by the fact that stroke prevalence increases with age, and as we age, the thirst signal (Phillips, et al., 1985) is not as strong as in youth. As a curiosity, the day before my stroke, while playing doubles tennis, a lady said to me, "Jim, you do not drink enough water." Yipes!

Published reports surrounding dehydration as related to stroke are fairly common but are not widely quoted. For example, "The Hydration Influence on the Risk of Stroke (THIRST) Study" (Rodriguez, et al., 2009) concluded that "elderly patients presenting with acute ischemic stroke or transient ischemic attack have high plasma osmolality[10] levels, suggestive of volume depletion. This seems to be an early phenomenon and possibly a contributing factor to cerebral ischemia."[11]

---

10   Osmolality is a test that measures the concentration of all chemical particles found in the fluid part of blood.

11   Cerebral Ischemia: Brain ischemia, also known as cerebral ischemia, is a condition in which there is insufficient blood flow to the brain to meet metabolic

Friedrich Manz et al. (2007) stated in his report, "Hydration and Disease", that "Hemoconcentration, Polycythemia, and Travel Thrombosis are risk factors for thromboembolism[12] that are possibly intensified by dehydration." He also noted "after acute ischemic stroke, venous thromboembolism was increased in patients with serum osmolality values more than 297 mosm/kg," and that in vitro tests show that changes in hydration can significantly impact adhesion, causing normal erythrocytes (red cells) to display adhesive properties similar to those of sickle cells.

It is more than just another pretty fact that according to the Texas Heart Institute Information Center, "even a moderate elevation in red blood cell count can be a risk factor for stroke. A high number of red blood cells thicken the blood, leading to blood clots."

Testing for Dehydration

One would think that all that is needed to clinch the stroke-dehydration question is to measure the hydration level in stroke victims as compared with hydration level of control patients. But here is the problem, captured by Armstrong (2007), titled *Assessing Hydration Status: The Elusive Gold Standard*. Although a significant number of test procedures have been used to reflect hydration status that range from simply noting the color of urine to one called direct-segmental bioelectrical impedance analysis (BIA) for measuring both intra- and extra-cellular water achieves 96 to 97 percent accuracy when compared against hydrostatic weighing (according to Powers et al. 2009), using bedside BIA for measuring total body water. What complicates the problem is that in the first place, children for example, have a higher percentage of water than adults, with women having less water than men, and fat people more than thin—and morbidly obese individuals may have only 36 percent water. The older the body, the less water retained in the cells—ergo, wrinkles and dry skin. Arriving at an unambiguous assessment of hydration state for disease comparison probably accounts for the lack of solid data and demand. This leads to poor oxygen.

12   Thromboembolism: The blocking of a blood vessel by a blood clot dislodged from its site of origin.

any significant progress in assessing impact of dehydration on stroke in particular. Any number of biochemical assessments has been made, with none yielding unchallenged data that I could find. Due to the lack of hydration during sleep, the case for dehydration as a factor in stroke can be supported most convincingly by the observation that "strokes occur most frequently before noon" (Kelley-Hayes 1995). And in the work of Gusev et al. (2008), they point out that people with ischemic stroke had three variants of circadian patterns of viscosity and hematocrit, with peaks at 9:00 AM, 3:00 PM, and 9:00 PM. They mentioned that for some patients, a strong correlation between the time of stroke onset and circadian pattern was observed.

It is not a big jump to notice that dehydration is in lock step with urine output and fluid intake, of course. For goodness sakes, would it be so difficult to observe a cohort of well-hydrated subjects versus minimally hydrated subjects to settle the question? One immediate problem I see would be the loss of opportunity for scientists to offer new, complicated metabolic pathways and also the loss of pharmaceutical remedies to treat dehydration. A comprehensive study of hydration is needed for every disease facing mankind.

For those who awaken at night to urinate on multiple occasions, **it can be said with confidence that without water consumption, the source of fluid for urine production is satisfied only by dehydration.** Part of this equation is also related to sleep quality, since our metabolism is more active if we are only at a shallow level of sleep; the more metabolically active at rest, the more urine output. **It is thus clear that dehydration associated with nocturnal toilet habits also could easily help explain why strokes occur more often before noon** (Partinen, 1995). (Emphasis mine.)

As previously discussed, it is entirely feasible that the relative concentration of the clotting pro-enzyme fibrinogen/red cell relationship is distorted by dehydration, thus inviting increased opportunity for red cell and platelet aggregation-associated clot formation and subsequent migration to brain, leading to stroke or migration to the heart, leading to heart attack.

Seen as a total package, the published data surrounding dehydration seems to be sufficiently compelling that a serious effort to produce an appropriately controlled study must be considered, if that is what it takes to get the attention of the stroke and heart attack-management industry. (If our vascular research institutions fail to do these studies, then we'd better start looking at the money trail for the reason.) What this is really saying is that maybe it is time to let some common sense prevail in the selection of our national research targets.

If one is looking for supporting evidence for dehydration contributing to stroke, there is a rather compelling geographic pattern of stroke in America. I am referring to the **stroke belt** that extends through the southeastern states, as previously mentioned. When you think about this pattern of stroke as possibly related to dehydration, it is easy to justify this clustering of stroke. The fact that those states are characterized as both hot and humid creates the environment for excessive perspiration and thus increased dehydration potential. Of course, there are other factors that enter the picture, such as the increased percentage of the population who are African Americans.

As described in another section of the book, a case is made for higher stroke risk in African Americans due to their propensity for sickle cell; this adds another layer of risk to that population according to the hypothesis developed around the schematic. Since there does not seem to be any clustering of stroke in hot, dry areas of the United States, one can guess that intuitively those living in that area know they must consume more water, which has become a natural part of their lifestyle.

So there you have it, as I see the picture. Those who live in hot, humid areas will get dehydrated more readily than those living in temperate zones and thus are more vulnerable to stroke.

But wait a minute: if this is true, then we should expect a similar cluster of heart attacks in the stroke belt. Checking into that point of view, I did come across the notation by a public service bulletin by Health Key referring to the CDC Behavioral Risk Factor Surveillance System (BRFSS) stating "Ongoing (telephone) survey by the Center for Disease Control indicate that people in some regions of the US—

particularly the Southeast—have a higher risk of chronic heart disease because of various social and economic factors." This bulletin, as quoted, did not specifically distinguish between stroke and heart attack rates, but the implication is there, as a starting place for anyone wishing to pursue more details.

Insulin Resistance

A riddle wrapped in a mystery inside an enigma—the entire Churchill catastrophe. Yes, we are talking about insulin resistance, and from what I can discern, we simply do not seem to know what in the world we are talking about. The problem relates to our definition of what purpose a measurement of A1C serves us. Let's start with how and why it is currently measured.

When glucose is absorbed into the bloodstream, some of it is picked up by the hemoglobin in red blood cells. This glycated (glucose-carrying) hemoglobin holds on to the glucose until the red blood cells die in about 120 days. The more glucose in the blood, the more glucose is carried by the hemoglobin. A direct correlation exists between blood glucose level and glycated hemoglobin, which is measured to determine the A1C level.

Insulin resistance, aside from depleting magnesium, as a partner of diabetes, is an important stroke risk factor. About 40 percent of the "normal" population are, in fact, insulin-resistant. It is my contention that if a subject is insulin-resistant, the door is open for nerve damage of the diabetes type. In fact, I predict that anyone who craves sweets is already insulin-resistant or on the path. One of the things I found that happens after a stroke is to continually test yourself by asking such things as, "Why do my stroke symptoms seem to ebb and flow with no apparent provocation?" As a case in point, at twenty-three months post-stroke, in spite of everything I had tried to accelerate recovery, nothing seemed to have any effect. I began to question why my symptoms of peripheral neuropathy—numbness in the left foot, hand, and calf, and gradual loss of functionality seemed so much more pronounced on some days than others. I continually searched for clues, starting most notably from my observation that if I consumed any high-glycemic food such as sugar, often within minutes, my left foot, calf, and hand would feel significantly more numb, cold, and swollen (although visually unchanged). This observation, repeatedly noted, usually subsided within a few hours or by morning awakening. These events led me to question whether I could possibly be experiencing a coincident diabetic neuropathy exacerbated in stroke-affected limbs. Since my neurologic symptoms seemed to perfectly parallel those described for diabetes, I began a study of a possible stroke-insulin resistance association. A quick check of the literature revealed the astounding fact that insulin resistance affects nearly one half of all patients with stroke or TIA (Kubetin 2002; Kernan, 2000). Insulin resistance (IR) is one of the signatures of diabetes, and surprising to me, affects up to 40 percent of apparently healthy subjects (NINDS IRIS, 2005) study. One of the major elements leading to stroke is how blood sugar is managed as related to insulin resistance and diabetes.

However, in my opinion, there is a flaw in the interpretation of insulin-resistance data that is having a significant impact on how we deal with it, and its subsequent partner, seen as diabetes. It all begins with the tool that is used to assess the status of our path to diabetes. I am referring to the test called HBA1C.

HBA1C Test

One of the most common tests for how well our bodies deal with sugar is the HBA1C test or A1C[13] for short. And what in the world does this have to do with the price of turnips? The efficiency of how well our bodies utilize sugar is expressed in terms of A1C values. And why is that of interest? Well, it turns out from studies of diabetes that excess sugar in our blood will attach to red cells and remain there for the life of the cell, which is commonly accepted to be four months. This means that if you can measure how much sugar is attached to red cells (and a

---

13   The A1C test (also known as HBA1C glycated hemoglobin or glycosylated hemoglobin) is a good general measure of diabetes care. While conventional home glucose monitoring measures a person's blood sugar at a given moment, the A1C test indicates a person's average blood glucose level over the past few months.

lab can), you will know what the average sugar load was during the last four months…a rather neat trick. The higher the A1C value was, the more sugar on average that was floating around. The A1C value often is used to decide whether a body is insulin-resistant, meaning on its way to diabetes.

But here is the rub: experts cannot decide what level of A1C constitutes a "normal" value. So it appears that anyone interested may decide what to consider a normal value. Let me give you some examples.

The ADA (American Diabetes Association) states A1C should be 7 percent or below; the AACE (American Association of Clinical Endocrinologists) stays with 6.5 percent or below; and most others state 7 percent or below. However, in the EPIC-Norfolk study (2006), they showed that an increase of 1 percent (6 percent as opposed to 5 percent) represented an increased risk of cardiovascular death of 28 percent higher. If I understand this right, you can see that selection of the normal value could have high impact on associated risk. Within each of the recommendations, they say that the A1C should be as low as possible without hypoglycemia,[14] and that coexisting health conditions must be factored in. The major testing laboratories usually say the "normal" range is 4.0 to 6.0 percent.

But get this: Bernstein, in his *The Diabetes Solution* (2007), indicated that as far as he has been able to determine, a truly normal HBA1C ranges from 4.2 to 4.6, a huge difference—or so it seems to me. So take your pick. In my case, I had an A1C of 5.7 when tested about thirty months post-stroke. By most standards, that would not implicate insulin resistance, but by Bernstein standards, it sure would. So I concluded that insulin resistance could not be ruled out for purposes of my neuropathy hypothesis, as discussed later.

What does all of this have to do with heart attack and stroke? Those who are insulin-resistant are known to feature depleted magnesium levels. Why is that important? Well, for starters, magnesium is critical

---

14   Hypoglycemia: An abnormally low level of glucose in the blood below-normal levels of blood glucose, quickly reversed by administration of oral or intravenous glucose.

for prevention of red cell auto-clumping. Without adequate magnesium, the clumped cells are more capable of clot formation and migration to the heart or brain. But here is another zinger: magnesium depletion is also associated with arrhythmia, which in its ultimate pathologic form, manifests as atrial fibrillation[15] (A Fib). Thus it is easy to see why that although it is A Fib that is called the risk factor, **it appears that before that, probably came magnesium depletion, and before that, probably insulin resistance.**

Insulin Purpose

The primary purpose of insulin is to control how the body converts and stores the sugar we eat. Insulin can be thought of as an escort to help sugar gain entry into the types of cells that need it to convert sugar into energy. Not all cells need this help, however, so that whereas muscle, liver, and fat cells must rely on insulin, other cells such as brain, kidney, and red blood cells do not. The amount of insulin needed by the body is related to the amount of sugar in the bloodstream; the higher the sugar load, the more insulin level. So what happens if sugar gets out of control? Well, that is where insulin resistance enters the picture.

Resistance to Insulin

Too much of anything can be toxic for our bodies. A perfect example is the effect of too much sugar in our diet, resulting in too much of it floating around in our bodies, and then followed by too much insulin. One result is that receptive proteins are able to combine with the glucose to form chemical complexes called Advanced Glycation End (AGEs) products by a process known as the Maillard reaction (Vertijl et al., 2000). This reaction is recognized in several ways. For example, as foods are cooked, they often assume a brown color (for example, fried potatoes). In our bodies, the accumulation of these complexes can contribute to age-related increase in lens crystals implicated in cataracts, and to the brown spots noticed on the back of the aging hand. So too,

15   Atrial Fibrillation: (AF or A-fib) is the most common cardiac arrhythmia (abnormal heart rhythm) and involves the two upper chambers of the heart.

with prolonged presence of AGEs comes a decrease in elasticity of skin and connective tissue collagens.[16] The browning reaction is also implicated in age-related diseases such as diabetes, atherosclerosis, and Alzheimer's disease. AGEs also lead to oxidative inflammatory changes associated with plaque accumulation in vascular diseases.

Every way you look at it, excess sugar in our diet is a bad actor, and in my opinion, should be thought of as a poison. As discussed above, the more sugar that enters our diet, the more insulin that is produced to control it, and ultimately the insulin itself rises to a toxic level. This is when we develop resistance to insulin. When this happens, the body no longer can produce insulin fast enough to compensate for the accumulating sugar that cannot get into the cells that need it to produce energy. The body responds by signaling a need for even more sugar which shows up as a craving—and thus begins the endless cycle that earns the name of type 2 diabetes.

To complicate matters even more is the fact that as we age, just like some of our senses and our awareness of thirst decline, so too the process of aging by itself also is at work to reduce insulin sensitivity. Thus, just by our nature, we must face the prospect that insulin resistance is just waiting to be discovered in our aging bodies. One would think this reality would be enough for our primary care physicians to include a test for insulin resistance in routine annual physical exams. From my experience, doctors who are alert to this need are in a small minority (although this could be a Medicare issue). Given the strong association between diabetes and stroke—accumulating this knowledge should become high priority in health care strategy.

Putting some of the effects of insulin in a brighter light, those who live beyond one hundred years have three important things in common: they have low blood sugar, low triglycerides, and low insulin, with the level of insulin sensitivity the most important marker of lifespan. Or put another way: Controlling insulin is one of the most powerful anti-aging strategies you can possibly implement. It all starts with sugar consumption control. This requires that you eliminate high-glycemic

---

16   Collagens: The fibrous protein constituent of bone, cartilage, tendon, and other connective tissue. It is converted into gelatin by boiling.

foods from your diet and that you understand the role and need for adequate magnesium in your diet, as described shortly.

To amplify some of these thoughts, we recognize that our bodies have met and solved all sorts of biochemical challenges for millennia, so they long ago provided a defense for controlling excess sugar with the hormone insulin. Each time we eat, insulin is released into our tissues to help convert sugar into energy as quickly as possible, or at least convert it into a less harmful storage form called glycogen. When the storage capacity for glycogen is exceeded, the glucose is stored as saturated fat (usually abdominal). As our pancreas produces an increased level of insulin to meet the otherwise toxic sugar load, the level of insulin itself rises to a toxic level. In an effort to protect itself, the body developed a strategy to make the cells resistant to the signal given by insulin to convert more glucose into energy. The liver cells are the first to become resistant, followed by muscle tissue, then fat cells.

As resistance to insulin increases at the same time as demand for insulin is high, all hell breaks loose as the body becomes diabetic. This path is now termed insulin resistance, Syndrome X, or metabolic syndrome. Those terms are invoked when a combination of risk factors for type 2 diabetes occurs. These factors usually involve chronically elevated insulin, low HDL,[17] abdominal obesity, and high blood pressure.

Syndrome X often is found in families with a history of early heart disease. Some of the symptoms of IR are said to be fatigue, poor memory, agitation, or depression, along with the increased blood pressure and fasting insulin level.

Hang on to your hat now: here is another confounding fact that will curl your hair. Insulin plays a role in the storage of magnesium, and if you are insulin-resistant, your critically important magnesium supply literally goes down the toilet (Rundek, 2008). To review the many faces of magnesium, you may want to have a careful look at Appendix IV on nutrients and supplements. You will note that claims for magnesium include the fact that magnesium deficit causes constriction of blood

---

17   HDL: High-density lipoprotein (HDL), a type of lipoprotein that protects against coronary artery disease.

vessels leading to elevated blood pressure, sticky red cells, and platelets, and also to arrhythmia which is associated with TIAs and stroke. This is especially crucial when coupled with dehydration, in my opinion.

On the other hand, if you cannot ever produce enough insulin, it will lead to type 1 diabetes, where the only way to cope is to receive injections of insulin.

If you have excess sugar or excess insulin in the blood vessels, being very toxic, they will damage several organs and tissues. These problems then morph into full-blown diabetes, where kidneys, eyes, and nerves are damaged, leading to blindness, kidney failure, and amputation of limbs—a nasty picture to be avoided at all costs.

So what to do to restore insulin function? Well, the first line of defense is usually to avoid sugar consumption.

There are drugs said to be helpful in restoring insulin sensitivity, and I refer you to one of the most authoritative books on the subject I know of, called *Syndrome X* by Gerald Reaven (2000). Reaven is credited with discovery of the metabolic syndrome also known as Syndrome X. Here, he offers dietary advice on how to manage insulin resistance.

Along this line, another must-have reference for diabetes management is found in the outstanding book by Bernstein titled *The Diabetes Solution*. This fine book was written by a clinician who has had diabetes for more than forty years and who has single-handedly turned the diabetes-management world right side up with his insightful analysis and problem solutions. Anyone needing advice on how to manage type 1 or type 2 diabetes will find this a comprehensive and compelling how-to manual.

My interpretation of the literature is that Bernstein is correct. Within his text is described his idea of a true normal value range for A1C: 4.2–4.6. This immediately distinguishes his work from all of the recognized authorities on diabetes. Bernstein made a huge contribution to understanding the dynamics of this epidemic.

But wait, there is more: according to Thompson and Barnes in their 2008 book called *The Calcium Lie,* they assert that early type 2 diabetes is treatable and reversible simply by increasing sodium intake in the form of rock or sea salt, along with what they describe as ionic mineral supplement. I suggest you consult their book for details.

To conclude this story, I re-emphasize that the problem with insulin resistance is that as the body senses elevated blood sugar, it in turn signals the need for more insulin, which then depletes the sugar. The body then starts craving sugar—and the cycle repeats itself endlessly, driving our bodies towards Type 1 or Type 2 diabetes.

As the final solution to a clogged sink is to run a sewer tape down it to restore maximum flow of waste, so too you must think of restoring sugar management by sending all excess sugar down the drain: do not eat it first. Let sugar go where it belongs—down the sewer. So long cake, pie, candy. This includes desserts of all types and stripes, colas, soda, energy drinks, and maybe even catsup, as it has a fair amount of sugar. By the way, did you ever notice that the winning barbeque recipe usually has the highest sugar content?

As mentioned elsewhere, if you crave sweets, you are probably already insulin-resistant or on the path. All the things insulin resistance can lead to, including stroke and heart attack are not a pretty scene. I also know you can lead a horse to water but you cannot make him drink. **A one-hour stroke experience would convince you to listen up *now*, to say nothing of carrying that burden for the rest of your life. Drink at least the recommended daily allowance of water and skip the sweets. It is just about that simple once your blood pressure is under control.**

Fibrinogen

Within the general thesis of a stroke-dehydration relationship, one of the most powerful players is the role of fibrinogen.[18] Wilhelmsen et al., (1984) published a paper on fibrinogen as a risk factor for stroke and heart attack. They concluded that, "although causality cannot be inferred from these data, it is possible that the fibrinogen level plays an important part in the development of stroke and myocardial infarction."

---

18   Fibrinogen: A protein produced by the liver. This protein helps stop bleeding by helping blood clots to form.

This speculation has been amplified and confirmed numerous times. For example, M. L. Bots et al. (1979) analyzing EUROSTROKE data concluded that, "Fibrinogen is a powerful predictor of stroke". In 1994, the authors stated that "during the last decade, several epidemiological studies have reliably demonstrated that plasma fibrinogen is a strong and independent risk factor for cardiovascular disease." They go on to observe that "the risk of developing a cardiovascular event such as ischemic heart disease or stroke, is 1.8 to 4.1 times higher in subjects with fibrinogen levels in the top third than those with levels the lower third." S.C. Kofoed et al. (2003) quoted data from 8,755 subjects that "suggest a doubling in risk of ischemic stroke for high verses low fibrinogen."

Stress Hormones

Stress hormones, as commonly recognized, usually reference the fight-or-flight response. Rolef Ben-Shahar (1998) describing the fight-or-flight response, points to adrenalin (also known as epinephrine), "as secreted by the adrenal glands in direct reaction to stressful situations." Notation was also made that "adrenalin is also an excitatory neurotransmitter in the central nervous system, indirectly controlling its own production."

Also mentioned was that during preparation for fight or flight, there is:

- Increased heart rate, blood pressure, and respiration.
- Increased sugar in the blood.
- Thickening of the blood by platelets, to stop bleeding quickly.
- Secretion of body wastes to make the body lighter.

Shown in Table 2 are the effects of stress and compensating hormones.

Table # 2: Effects of Stress and Compensating Hormones	
Physiologic Responses of Our Body to Cortisol and Adrenalin	**Physiologic Responses of our Bodies to Oxytocin**
Aggression	Reduced anti-social behavior
Arousal	Calming
Anxiety	Increased curiosity
Addiction	Reduced cravings
Decreased libido	Increased sexual receptivity
Brain cells affected by toxicity	Positive feelings
Breakdown of muscles/bones/joints	Accelerated repair, healing, restoration
Depressed immune system	Positive feelings
Increased pain	Diminished pain
Clogging of arteries	Cardiac protection
Heart Disease	Reduced stress
High Blood Pressure	Lowered Blood Pressure
Obesity	
Diabetes	
Osteoporosis	

You may want to keep these responses in mind, because the increased blood sugar associated with stress plays importantly into the insulin resistance story, and into the hypothesis for neuropathy discussed.

In a report by Black and Garbutt (2002), they state "inflammatory events, caused by stress, may account for the approximately 40 percent of atherosclerotic patients with no other known risk factors. Stress, by activating the sympathetic nervous system, the hypothalamic-pituitary axis, and the renin-angiotensin system, causes the release of various stress hormones such as catecholamines, corticosteroids, glucagon, growth hormone, and renin, and elevated levels of homocysteine, which induce a heightened state of cardiovascular activity, injured endothelium, and induction of adhesion molecules on endothelial cells to which recruited inflammatory cells adhere and translocate to the arterial wall. An acute phase response (APR), similar to that associated with inflammation, is also engendered, which is characterized by macrophage activation, the production of cytokines, other inflammatory mediators, acute phase proteins (APPs), and mast cell activation, all of which promote the inflammatory process. Stress also induces an atherosclerotic lipid profile with oxidation of lipids and, if chronic, a hypercoagulable state that may result in arterial thrombosis. Shedding of adhesion molecules and the appearance of cytokines, and APPs in the blood are early indicators of a stress."

Inflammation-induced Arrhythmia

A key feature of this thesis is the proposition that A and AF are products of inflammation, and that each of the agents shown in the schematic is in fact, capable of causing inflammation.

Diabetes is a serious (epidemic) disease where, because of the lack of a particular hormone, certain foods we eat (such as sugar) accumulates in our blood, rather than being changed into energy or fat. **High sugar in our blood can cause blood to clot**. The reason for this discussion is to offer a possible mechanism for clot formation in AF events that does not rely on an erratic heartbeat, and thus may offer a possible explanation why not all AF events lead to heart attack or stroke. Doctors and patients need to understand this difference so they can make appropriate changes in their health habits to help avoid these two diseases.

From this discussion, it should be evident that the most important changes we can make are to drink more water and to be sure we have good nutrition, including a diet rich in magnesium such as nuts, seeds, whole grains, and legumes. In my opinion, it is highly unlikely that clots are caused by Plavix deficiency or the like.

Red Cell Clotting Mechanisms
and Working Backward

New way blood flow to brain or heart compromised

This proposed stroke and heart and heart attack mechanism, offers a second method by which blood flow can be blocked in a way that would resemble clot formation. There are several ways shown in the schematic where red cells can aggregate to form potential agents for blood blockage. The novel part of this proposal is that with this idea, comes a possible explanation of why Coumadin, for example, is not 100 percent effective in preventing future stroke or heart attack events. Red cell agglutinating agents do not rely on the fibrinogen-mediated formation of clots typically associated with S and HA. Thus from this perspective new approaches to management of these diseases involving prevention of cell aggregation could be a worthy goal.

The following eight agents represent proposed mechanisms by which red cells could (in theory) lead to clot formation and then migrate to heart or brain, causing a heart attack or embolic stroke. The list is not meant to exclude other possible microbial, physical, or chemical agents.

Starting with the general hypothesis that dehydration could contribute to the cause of stroke, one way to uncover support for the notion is to work backward into the problem. Thinking from that direction, I have tried to find evidence in published reports that could lend support. Starting with the accepted proposition that migrating blood clots are central to the mechanism, I first questioned why unwanted clots form in the first place. I found that there are several reasons why clots could form and then migrate to the brain. If the body is sufficiently dehydrated, one could easily imagine how an unusual blood-chemistry shift could change the normal pattern of red cell and platelet association with fibrinogen balance with nothing more needed.

Quite apart from any speculation, one can look at diseases known to affect properties of red cells and see whether the incidence of stroke is changed in those populations. Batmanghelidj's book is a must-read for a full review of the scope of the dehydration problem.

There are three keys to understanding the crucial role of adequate hydration:

1. As we age, we gradually experience sensory loss, which manifests as hearing and sight loss, as well as a reduction in thirst, taste, and libido.
2. Drinking fluids is not the same as drinking water, as many popular beverages—including coffee, alcohol, and sodas—actually contribute to dehydration.
3. The body seems to allocate water, so the brain for example, gets first dibs. However, over the years, the effects of chronic water shortage are so insidious it may be hard to spot them until a disease shows up.

I scanned numerous general-health texts to make note of the frequency with which dehydration was identified as an associated cause of disease. If mentioned at all, it was usually as related to constipation, cataracts, or macular degeneration. Dehydration was not even in the index of most of the health-related texts that I viewed. Batmanghelidj seems to have it right, as inferred from him. Dehydration in health management is seldom a consideration.

Influenza Virus

Influenza infection is one of several mechanisms by which clots could form, leading to stroke. Influenza virus is capable of agglutinating[19] red cells. An excellent account of the temporal relationship between influenza infections and subsequent first-ever stroke incidence was published in *Age and Aging* by Oxford University Press on behalf of the British Geriatrics Society in 2008. Among their findings was the notation that, "Multivariate analysis of the influenza and ischemic stroke time series yielded a significant association between influenza and first-ever strokes when they occur within a time lag of one week

---

19   Agglutinating: To cause substances, such as bacteria, to clump together.

and two weeks. For a time lag more than two weeks, no significant association (with stroke) could be observed." Powerful support for this thesis is found in numerous reports showing a reduced stroke risk in influenza-vaccinated subjects.

These observations were of particular interest to me in the context of my study of the literature, since the influenza/stroke correlation reported occurred within an interval where a viremia[20] would be expected, and lasted until a viremia likely would have abated. In the British report, however, correlation with hemorrhagic-type stroke occurred only within four weeks after infection. This suggests a different mechanism from a virus-mediated agglutination of red cells contributing to stroke etiology herein proposed. Considering the former referred to ischemic and the latter to hemorrhagic stroke, the pattern is reasonable and expected.

Here is where the influenza connection gets more interesting: In the 2009 paper by Lipsitch and Viboud entitled *Influenza Seasonality: Lifting the Fog,* they state that, "Influenza is perhaps the seasonal disease of most profound interest, because it is responsible for much of the seasonal variation in other infectious and noninfectious causes of morbidity and mortality. Influenza virus activity display strong seasonal cycles in temperate areas of the world, and less defined seasonality in tropical regions."

Viboud, Alonso, and Simonsen (2006) write, "In temperate regions, there is clear seasonal variations in the occurrence of influenza, **with a peak in cold winter months**." (Emphasis mine.)

To provide a broad view of the possible relationship between influenza infection and stroke, consider too, the study provided by the American Heart/Stroke Association written in 1995, referring to the Framingham study titled, *Temporal Patterns of Stroke Onset,* in which they state, "**Winter was the peak season for cerebral embolic stroke.** (Emphasis mine.) Significantly more stroke events occurred on Mondays than any other day, particularly for working men. For intracerebral hemorrhages, a third happened on Mondays in both genders.

"**The time of day when strokes most frequently occurred was between 8:00 AM and noon. This pattern was true for all stroke subtypes**." (Emphasis mine.)

---

20   Viremia: The presence of viruses in the bloodstream.

I am not suggesting that influenza virus infection per se is a significant cause for stroke; the discussion is more to point out the possibility that a heme-agglutinating type of agent could provide a mechanism for clot formation ultimately associated with embolic stroke, especially when coupled with dehydration.

Chlamydia

There is a history of an association between chlamydia and cardiovascular and other diseases. Since it is not my intent to produce a review of the subject, representative studies include: Campbell, Kuo, and Grayston, entitled "Chlamydia pneumonia and cardiovascular Disease" (1998) published in *Emerging Infectious Diseases* (Vol.4 No.4, Oct–Dec 1998) and another by KF & KM Poehlmann (Copyright 2002–05), entitled "Chlamydia Linked to Heart Disease, Stroke, and Alzheimer's."

Here are some of the features of Chlamydia:
- Considered nanobacteria, thus among the smallest of all bacteria.
- Question whether they are living entities or are crystals of calcium carbonate.

Two genetically different strains of concern:
- Pneumoniae: a mild form of pneumonia followed by a long-term infection.
- Trachomatis: the sexually transmitted form of chlamydia.

According to Poehlmann, **C. pneumoniae is a major factor in stroke, dementia, heart disease, and arterial sclerosis.** (Emphasis mine.) On the other hand, Campbell, Kuo, and Grayston, as published in 1998, were more cautious, concluding; "A causative role of *C. pneumoniae* infection in cardiovascular disease has not yet been firmly established. However, the high frequency of infection found in human atherosclerotic tissue in comparison to normal tissue, the induction and progression of atherosclerotic-like inflammatory changes in infected animal models of atherosclerosis, and the early results from antichlamydia intervention studies in humans are consistent with a causative role of *C. pneumoniae* in the disease process." Also, Apfalter, as an editorial, wrote of *Chlamydia pneumoniae,* stroke, and serological associations (2006). From the Northern Manhattan Stroke Study is the work of Elklind, Lin, Grayston, and Sacco (1998). This documentation is supplied in support of the schematic shown in Chapter Three.

Mycoplasma

As another example of red cell agglutination, in terms of stroke, there is a relationship between mycoplasma infection and stroke. Mycoplasma are red cell-agglutinating agents, and although not numerous, there are scattered reports linking mycoplasma with stroke (Fu, et al., 1998; Ngeh, et al., 2005; and Grau, et al., 2005). I am not suggesting this is a major stroke partner; I merely propose that the findings are consistent with a stroke-agglutination mechanism.

In terms of mycoplasma infection and stroke, Joseph Ngeh and Colin Goodbourne (2005) wrote that "the risk of stroke/TIA appears to be associated with the aggregate number of chronic infectious burden of atypical respiratory pathogens such as *C. pneumoniae, M. pneumoniae,* and *L. Pneumophilia.*"

A. J. Grau et al. (1995) in their paper, *Recent Infection as a Risk Factor for Cerebrovascular Ischemia,* stated that "Bacterial infections dominated among patients but not among control subjects. Infection increased the risk for cerebrovascular ischemia in all age groups; this reached significance for patients aged 51 to 60, and 61 to 70 years. Infection remained a significant risk factor when previous stroke, hypertension, diabetes mellitus, coronary heart disease, and current smoking, were included as covariate in a logistic model (OR, 4.6; 95 percent CI, 1.9 to 11.3)."

Sickle Cell

Sickle cell anemia is a condition that influences red cell integrity and cell-to-cell association. Checking stroke incidence, one finds definite evidence of increased stroke risk associated with sickle cell anemia.

Verduzco and Nathan, in their 2009 report, state that 24 percent of sickle cell disease (SCD) patients have a stroke by age forty-five. In the American Heart Association information sheet *Learn and Live,* it is stated that "children with SCD are 221 times more likely to suffer stroke. It also is known that sickle cell is associated with dehydration."

Rheumatoid Arthritis

Reasoning that agglutination of red cells has been used to test for evidence of rheumatoid arthritis (RA), one also can find ample evidence of increased stroke risk among those affected by rheumatoid arthritis.

Examples of studies connecting RA with cardiovascular diseases may be found in the work of Gonzalis-Gay et al. (2005) in their paper, *Rheumatoid Arthritis: A Disease Associated with Accelerated Atherogenesis,* and in the work of Van Doornum et al. (2006), *Reducing the Cardiovascular Disease Burden in Rheumatoid Arthritis.* Also in *Therapy Insight: Managing Cardiovascular Risk in Patients with Rheumatoid Arthritis* by Giles et al. (2006). Additional studies include *Cardiovascular Risk in Rheumatoid Arthritis* by Nurmohamed (2009) and the 2006 review by Kaplan. Reference to dehydration in the RA group also was noted by Batmanghelidj.

The Stroke-Shingles Connection

Herpes virus is not usually thought of as a hemeagglutinating type of virus, however there is an interesting connection between shingles (a herpes infection), and an elevated stroke risk. If you Google shingles and stroke, you will find several references to a 30% increase in stroke risk in subjects with shingles. I refer to the account found at http://www.physorg.com/news174245586.html retrieved on 4/28/2011. This is a report by Kang et al., which is peer-reviewed evidence.

Shingles is caused by Varicella zoster, the virus causing chicken pox. Since the mechanism for its relationship with stroke is unknown, it is fair to point out that this relationship fits nicely with my proposed stroke mechanism flow diagram and with my neuropathy hypothesis with a modest caveat. In the report cited by Kang, they stated, "people treated for shingles infection were thirty one percent more likely to have a stroke, compared with patients without a shingles infection."

According to my neuropathy hypothesis, it is possible that the drug used to treat the shingles patients, was itself neurotoxic and could have caused what could be called a reactivation of herpes virus. If that is true there would be a likely measurable viremia in treated but not in control subjects. Thus maybe it was the drug that started the cascade. As a second avenue that could explain the stroke connection, it is possible that reactivated virus mediated by antibody, favored the clumping of red cells leading to clot formation that leads to stroke.

To expand slightly, the shingles-stroke relationship, now calls into question whether the red cell agglutinating agents shown in the schematic, may actually be a case where those microbes are operating in the presence of their specific antibodies. In that context, antibodies could attach to red cells with the microorganisms serving as a bridge to lock red cells together. For anyone who may want to notice this idea for further study, I think it would be important to determine if the ABO blood types possibly facilitate the attachment of antibody to the red cells. Whatever the case, the entire scenario still fits well with the neuropathy hypothesis whereby a neurotoxic agent can reactivate a latent microorganism providing the bridge for red cell association, and thus to stroke or heart attack.

Does this imply that rheumatoid arthritis, or that sickle cell for example, actually may have an unknown microbial or antigenic component? Humm.

The Stroke-Antibody Angle is a Sticky Wicket

This potential stroke mechanism involving antibody-coated red cells offers a new research target. Given that 20 percent of the population caries a latent herpes virus, we should find out, if not known, if the frequency of herpes antibody is disproportionate among stroke and heart attack subjects. Maybe a latent virus is not so innocent when it comes to S and HA risks factors

Magnesium

The crucial and varied applications for magnesium in our biochemistry are numerous as partially listed in the nutrients/supplements section of this book (Appendix VI).

In terms of magnesium's relationship to stroke: magnesium has been found to help ward off formation of unwanted blood clots (minimize stickiness), lower blood pressure, prevent some of the complications related to diabetes, and limit effects of free radicals. Magnesium is needed for nerve transmission and is especially helpful in maintaining normal heart rhythm and restoring normal heartbeat pattern during episodes of arrhythmia (as I can personally testify). According to World Heart Federation Information Sheet 3-18-2010, the observation stated that there is inherited propensity toward sticky cells associated with lupus, RA, certain cancers, pregnancy, and vascular diseases predicts that each of these problems necessarily will be associated with increased risk for heart attack and stroke. Indeed, confirmation of that result was found in numerous publications.

Effects of Magnesium Deficiency

According to the Linus Pauling Institute of Oregon State University Information Sheet, "the following conditions are related to magnesium deficiency: prolonged diarrhea, Crohn's disease, malabsorption syndromes, celiac disease, diabetes mellitus, and chronic alcoholism. These all contribute to magnesium depletion. **Several studies have found that elderly people have relatively low dietary intakes of magnesium, and intestinal absorption tends to decrease with age, as urinary magnesium excretion tends to increase with age. This also fits well with the known increased stroke risk with age.** (Emphasis mine.)

The recommended dietary allowance for male adults is 400 mg/day and for females about 300 mg/day. In a magnesium supplement study, for three months at 800-1,200 mg/day, resulted in an average 35% reduction in platelet-dependent thrombosis which is a measure of the propensity of blood to clot.

25% to 38% of diabetics have been found to have decreased serum levels of magnesium, noting that one cause of the depletion may be associated with the increased urinary flow. Magnesium depletion has been shown to increase insulin resistance. (Emphasis mine.)

A double blind placebo controlled study in Type 2 diabetes found that those taking oral magnesium chloride at 12.5 mg/day for 26 weeks had improved measures of insulin sensitivity and glycemic control compared to placebo group."

Migraine Headache

Individuals with migraine headaches have lower intracellular magnesium, both in red and white cells. In other studies, increased stroke had been associated with migraine (Tzourio et al., 1995). It should be noted the Batmanghelidj also included migraine as a dehydration consequence.

Here is a reliable no-drug tip for wake-up headaches: We have discovered with a simple five-minute application of a Wal-Mart hand vibrator to neck, shoulders, and along spine to the tailbone, that those types of headaches are relieved immediately. I have not been able to test on a migraine subject, but the idea is offered if the reader wants to evaluate the method.

Here is a summary list of substances and conditions said to reduce body magnesium according to Krispin.com:

- Alcohol—all forms cause significant losses of magnesium
- Amphetamine/cocaine
- Chronic pain—any causes
- Coffee—causes significant loss
- Cyclosporine—extra magnesium may protect from side effects (any chance it would work for Cipro protection too?)
- Diabetes—magnesium spills with sugar into urine
- Diarrhea—any cause
- Dieting—stress

- Diuretics—even potassium-sparing diuretics do not spare magnesium
- High-glycemic carbohydrates
- High-levels of calcium will block magnesium absorption, as will zinc, I understand
- Insulin—whether using insulin or from hyperinsulinemia
- Large surface burns
- Old age
- Over training
- Phentermine/fenfluramine
- Sodas, especially cola type—both diet and regular
- Sodium—high salt intake
- Surgery
- Sweat

To summarize the rationale for my hypothesis, I have discussed the role of arrhythmia, the role of dehydration, and the role of fibrinogen as a co-player with dehydration. Then I showed evidence for various red cell agglutinating mechanisms that include influenza, mycoplasma infections, and sickle cell disease. This was concluded by showing how and why RA fits into the theory and how insulin resistance gets into the act.

CHAPTER FOUR

Neuropathy Hypothesis
"a work in progress"

Introduction

While documenting my stroke experience coupled with intensive literature searches over the past three years, a major departure from usual stroke thinking occurred. A hypothesis was developed showing a proposed mechanism explaining how and why neuropathies re-manifest following nerve injury. In addition, it explained why neuropathies may occur in some but not all subjects exposed to statins and other agents that have an affinity for nerve tissue.

The Hypothesis

I am hypothesizing that once a nerve supply is damaged by a neurologic event—whether chemical, biological, or physical—those nerves, if later exposed to a chemical, physical, or biological neurological agent, will respond with the appearance of exacerbated reaction to the original neuroinsult.

Having reviewed numerous stroke-related texts to learn what I could about embolic stroke, I found that the most vexing post-stroke issue I faced was not even mentioned in those accounts. I am referring to post-stroke peripheral neuropathy. For me, this appeared as a residual product of my embolic shower. The effects manifested only on the stroke-affected side of my body, with all of the symptoms that characterize diabetic neuropathy. Those symptoms include itching and burning, along with numbness in hand and foot. In addition, walking became increasingly compromised. To complicate matters a bit more, the weakened left leg muscles seemed unable to relax, resembling what I presume might be consistent with something in the Myotonia family of muscle issues, discussed shortly.

Exploring this pathway though this hypothesis first requires a fork in the road to bring insulin resistance (IR) into the picture. As a framework for introducing IR, I refer to the work of Kubetin (2002) and Kernan (2005) *reporting on the IRIS (Insulin Resistance Intervention after Stroke Trial) study, where it was stated that of 1,733 subjects who had screening blood work, 61 percent were insulin-resistant.* (Emphasis mine.) This hypothesis thus is an attempt to show how and why symptoms of a damaged nerve path can emerge in an exaggerated manner when exposed to a subsequent neurologic challenge. From the IRIS Study quoted, insulin resistance is commonly associated with stroke, so that the stage is set for symptoms of peripheral neuropathy (PN) to surface among stroke subjects, according to the hypothesis. There is one detail missing, and that is, that PN has not been clinically reported as significant among stroke subjects to my knowledge. I judge there must be yet other factor(s) involved in my particular case, such as perhaps I faced a combination of multiple neurologic challenges that preconditioned my nerve tissue, which stretches this too far into speculation to be useful.

Neuropathy was just described as a possible unrecognized product of stroke; now at 40 months post event 3-1-11, I still believe that is true but only in a very indirect way. Consistent with my neuropathy theory, I now believe that Coumadin could be neurotoxic and behave just like high blood sugar, reacting with previously damaged nerves causing them to manifest old neurologic symptoms (in this case preexisting occult diabetic neuropathy symptoms). This idea is not bizarre, since there are numerous internet references to neuropathy associated with Coumadin seemingly hidden from common knowledge. Here is an example: Written in eHealthMe (retrieved on 3-3-2011) they report that 0.14 percent of people taking Warfarin (Coumadin) have neuropathy. The interesting point they make is that according to age groups, 81.3

percent of those 60+ years have neuropathy when taking the drug. Given that stroke is concentrated among the elderly, this implies that there is a significant incidence of neuropathy among stroke subjects as I interpret their data. While I had viewed diabetic-type neuropathy as an unrecognized product of stroke, it now seems that the neuropathy is equally likely a result of the use of Coumadin.

In my case, I believe I must have been insulin-resistant (A1C-5.7) before the stroke, and the neuropathic events combined to manifest diabetic-type neuropathy, principally on the stroke-affected side of my body. Support for this notion comes from my observation of an instant and sometimes dramatic neurologic response that occurs associated with sugar consumption. Neuropathy is almost immediately exacerbated on the stroke-affected side of my body, and abates after a few hours. Neurologic reactivation has been observed in other diseases such as MS (Handel et al. 2009), reactivation of Epstein-Baar (Torkildsen, Nyland, and Myhr 2008), (Gutierrez et al. 2002), HHV-6 reactivation, and multiple sclerosis (Chapenko et al. 2003). Here is possible indirect symptomatic support for my hypothesis.

Post-Polio Syndrome

Post-polio syndrome (PPS), as described by Jubelt and Agre (2000), is a condition that affects polio survivors anywhere from ten to forty years after recovery from an initial paralytic attack of the poliomyelitis virus. PPS is characterized by a further weakening of muscles that were previously affected by the polio infection. Symptoms include fatigue, slowly progressive muscle weakness, and at times, muscular atrophy. Joint pain and increasing skeletal deformities such as scoliosis are common. Some patients experience only minor symptoms, while others develop spinal muscular atrophy, and very rarely, what appears to be, but is not, a form of amyotrophic lateral sclerosis (ALS), also called Lou Gehrig's disease. PPS is rarely life-threatening.

It seems to me that PPS easily could be a stroke or neurotoxic agent-induced phenomenon that quite neatly offers an explanation for the syndrome. It seems like MRIs of PPS patients should be studied for evidence of stroke lesions. It would be remarkable if that type of study never has been done, but who knows?

For purposes of illustration, one of the pathways into this hypothesis is provided by a careful look at sugar consumption and its effect on Polio.

Sugar Effect on Polio

Here is a short excursion into history that illustrates the potential role of sugar in neurologic disease.

I can recall a discussion with Albert Sabin in the late 50s while visiting our Pfizer Laboratories to discuss the production of his live oral polio vaccine. I remember how he described the influence of sugar on polio epidemics. It was his contention that polio epidemics occurred with the greatest frequency and severity in countries where sugar consumption was high compared with poor countries. He equated high sugar food consumption with countries that could afford luxury foods. He speculated that a correlation existed between wealthy countries and polio risk, which he attributed to sugar consumption. This observation by Sabin was in fact published in the Journal of American Medical Association in 1947 (see references) and is worth a new look by vascular scientists interested in this point of view.

This look at poliomyelitis as related to sugar consumption is powerful support for this hypothesis. Albert Sabin, the recognized father of live oral polio vaccine, is quoted in *JAMA*, June 1947 as follows: "Thus we see that sugar consumption is by far the greatest in the richer countries where one would also expect to find advanced sanitation and hygiene. Epidemics have occurred with the greatest frequency and severity in the high sugar consuming countries. *In fact, epidemics have never been reported in the natives of the low sugar consuming countries,* such as China." (Emphasis mine.) There are numerous additional sources of observations in this regard which can be found by Googling *polio sugar consumption.*

Dr. Sabin stated, *"No circumstance in the history of poliomyelitis is so baffling as its change during the past 50 years from a sporadic to an epidemic disease." An increasing consumption of sugar, as shown in his (updated table below), helps explain this change in the incidence of the disease.* (Emphasis mine.)

Table #1: Consumption Of Sugar In The United States	
Years	**Yearly Average Pounds Per Capita**
1880-1890	44*
1900-1910	65*
1920-1930	100*
2000	152**
	*Sugar Only **Total Caloric Sweeteners

Continuing from Sabin:

> The fact that polio has not been prevented by advanced sanitation and hygiene indicates that its incidence is controlled and influenced by factors quite different from the factors that bring about the spread of typhoid and the other diseases. As previously stated, advanced sanitation and hygiene are to be found in the richer countries, and one of the unfortunate evils that accompany wealth is the consumption of sugar in the form of luxury foods such as ice cream, candies, soft drinks, cakes, pies, pastries, and the like. Poor countries cannot afford luxury foods, sanitation, and hygiene. That is how I would explain the greater incidence of polio in countries with advanced sanitation and hygiene.

Interpreting Sabin's thoughts in light of this hypothesis shows that Dr. Sabin came within an eyelash of this full hypothesized picture. His observations fit perfectly into an explanation for polio epidemics resulting from nerve tissue damaged by excess sugar.

This possibility should set off alarms around the world, since our total caloric sweetener consumption is now up to 6.6 ounces per person per day, versus 2.0 in 1880. This dramatic increase in sugar consumption predicts that we will face an epidemic of neuromuscular diseases as the population ages. The time to interdict this process should start **now.**

The implication here is that high sugar consumption led to high blood sugar and that, in turn, to insulin resistance—a prescription for nerve damage that, in theory, preconditions the body for subsequent super-susceptibility to such an event as infection with poliomyelitis virus. According to this hypothesis, other neurological sequelae in addition to polio would also have manifest measurably more frequently in high sugar-consuming populations. By the way, an excellent account of the penalties and management of sugar consumption may be found in the book by Appleton (1995).

Quoting from the Center for Agriculture and Rural Development, Iowa State University (2005), "In the United States, the annual averages, per capita, for total caloric sweeteners in 1950–59 was 110 lbs. In the year 2000, it was 152 lbs. per capita (6.6 ounces per day)." The reference to 152 pounds used to update Sabin's table came from this source. The 6.6 ounces per day was my calculation.

African American Stroke Risk

The hypothesis presented herein easily leads to some interesting speculation, for example: African Americans (AA) have a known increased risk for sickle cell anemia (SCA). This is a disease characterized by "sticky red cells", as previously described. It is immediately tempting to put the notion of "preconditioned red cell" hypothesis to a test by predicting that a more accurate stroke and heart attack risk assessment for AAs could be calculated if we identified members of that cohort with and without known sickle cell. Those who are skilled in assessing public health risk can surely refine this idea and deliver a reliable statistical statement to account for the true difference in heart and stroke risk between AAs and Caucasians. That effort would go a long way in deciding the validity of the hypothesis. If the hypothesis is valid, those subjects with SCA will have a measurably higher incidence of stroke and heart attack.

Relapsing Form of Multiple Sclerosis

I noticed an advertisement in the Asheville Times on 4-19-11, recruiting subjects for evaluation of the drug Fingolimod, as related to Relapsing form of Multiple Sclerosis (RFMS).

This is the first time I have come across this syndrome, and call this to attention since it would seem to fit nicely into my Neuropathy Hypothesis as a test of validity. A brief Google search of Fingolimod revealed the following regarding its safety: given that disseminated Varicella zoster and herpes simplex encephalitis were apparently associated with use of this drug. This account seems to be describing a drug with an affinity for nerve tissue similar to drugs such as the statins and to the antibiotic Cipro. According to this theory, such chemical agents have the potential to reactivate latent viruses as discussed in detail previously.

If my theory is proven correct, it could provide regulating agencies a new tool to assess the safety of new drug applications.

A five minute Google search revealed the following regarding Fingolimod safety:

> Two deaths were seen during the TRANSFORMS study, both in the higher-dose group; 1 death was attributed to disseminated primary varicella zoster and the other to herpes simplex encephalitis. Other adverse events with fingolimod in that study included nonfatal herpes virus infections, skin cancer, and elevated liver enzymes.
>
> Retrieved on 4-22-2011
> http//www.medscape.com/viewarticle/729172

If my theory is correct, what we seem to have here, is another chemical agent with the potential to act like a statin or like the antibiotic Cipro with an attraction for nerve tissue. This, according to theory, could activate latent neurologic historic events such as varicella and herpes simplex depending on the immunologic history of the recipient of the drug.

What this is saying is that without knowing the specific history of every patient treated, there is a risk for fatality in those patients with neurovirus infections in their history. Is the money received for clinical evaluation of such a drug worth that level of responsibility? Relapsing forms of disease need more careful study to test this question. Based upon my neuropathy hypothesis, I predict that use of the drug, Fingolimod eventually will be found to increase stroke risk.

It is a damned shame our society is more interested in producing more new drugs to sell, whatever their risks, than to focus on prevention of disease.

FDA, NIH are you listening?

Myotonia

Although the sensation of tensed left thigh muscles became evident immediately post-stroke, it was not until about thirty months later (February 2010) that it dawned on me that this was significantly affecting mobility. While I had been able to walk with minimal support, I now had to stay close to a wall or furniture when moving, as the left leg was becoming progressively more rigid, forcing one step at a time sequence—not a fluid walking motion. There was notable hyper reflex with thigh muscle percussion, and the muscles were slow, or seemingly never to relax. It was in a parallel fashion to IR previously discussed, where I came to believe that I very likely had underlying insulin resistance that set the stage for a neurologic response to neurotoxins such as sugar. It was natural then for me to pick up that thread of thought and ask myself if I could possibly be experiencing yet another occult neurologic phenomenon that contained a tensed-muscle syndrome. This was brought to focus when I began to wonder why upon awakening that the usual refreshing body stretch was not productive. I realized I could not tense/stretch the left leg, because it was already tensed.

That is where that question led me once more through a literature search to myotonia and then to myotonic muscular dystrophy (MMD). The tensed muscles were also very evident when walking. My knee did not readily bend as it had even six months prior. Neither the ankle nor the foot would move unrestricted either, leaving me with an even more picturesque Herman Munster gait—stiff-legged with lateral steps combined with forward steps. You get the picture, I'm sure. This was beginning to get my goat, since my first reaction to this gradual change was that my stroke symptoms were probably a sign of progressive stroke—discussed later. In a sense, they were progressive stroke symptoms, but possibly one could look at this another way and picture that an occult form of MMD was just getting around to clearly manifest itself. Not really more stroke per se, but possibly just more uncovering of a latent hypothesized MMD, which also seemed to be exacerbated by sugar consumption.

I wanted to know if I could find support for my hypothesis that any peripheral neurologic disease could precondition nerves so that they became super-sensitive to future neurologic insult. I did, in fact, ask my primary care physician if he would consider having my blood tested for genetic evidence of MMD, for purposes of this book, at my expense.

Possible examples of this phenomenon are hypothesized to be associated with exposure to neurotoxins like statin drugs, the antibiotic Cipro, a neurovirus like herpes, or simple nutrients like sugar, elevated insulin, or of course, to an event like embolic stroke.

I found that Myotonic dystrophy[1] is the most commonly occurring form of MMD, appearing in one in eight thousand subjects, so it would not be a big surprise to carry that or a similar latent neurological affliction.

This hypothesis predicts that a disease like diabetes, manifesting neuropathy, will exhibit an exaggerated neurologic response if later taking a statin drug, an antibiotic like Cipro, or any other agent with neurologic sequelae.

Genetic Study

Genetic testing results from Wake Forest Molecular Genetic laboratory of 5-26-10 are quoted as follows: "Interpretation: negative result Myotonic dystrophy type 1 (DM1) analysis indicates James Crawford

---

1   Myotonic dystrophy is part of a group of inherited disorders called muscular dystrophies. It is the most common form of muscular dystrophy that begins in adulthood.

has a normal trinucleotide repeat range (allele sizes 14 and 5 within the myotonin protein kinase gene (DMPK)."

While it is gratifying to receive a negative report for myotonic dystrophy, it seems to me that genetic support for my hypothesis would still need a survey of other possible genetically related muscular afflictions such as myotonia congenita and reflex sympathetic dystrophy. Since I am not knowledgeable about neurologic diseases involving muscles—or anything else—I have relied on Internet study for my modest exposure to this subject. My goal will be to fill in the gaps by having additional genetic studies done if they seem appropriate for a later edition of this book.

Possible Secrets Held in Immune Globulin

There is yet another avenue to consider for providing potential support for this neuropathy hypothesis. This avenue of thought came about illegally, unfolding as follows.

A year in planning culminated in a one-week eastern Caribbean fun cruise in June of 2010, arranged by my wife Sylvia to include the families of all of my children and grandchildren, a total of sixteen members. The one caveat was that I had to pledge not to work on this manuscript while on the trip. Honoring that pledge, while I added no text to the book, it was impossible not to think about any element that might be useful to the overall book message—thus, these were nearly illegal thoughts, and only time will reveal if they prove to be significant.

Two or more years ago, RG, husband of daughter Cindy—members of our cruise family—experienced a debilitating neurologic response following a single dose of the antibiotic Cipro, prescribed for urinary tract infection in 2008 (which still persisted in 2010).

As research is my life, along with my stroke studies, I spent countless hours studying the Cipro problem, trying to uncover clues about cause and cure (unsuccessfully). His symptoms included a sensation of pins and needles. At this point, there are no published insights on a causal mechanism or a cure. As a highly successful basketball coach in New Mexico, a disability such as this can take the fun out being in contention or as state champions for much of the last twenty years.

Returning to the Cipro mechanism, it occurred to me that the RG syndrome could possibly be explained within the context of this theory if anything could be uncovered from his history that included a viral infection of a type that had the propensity for invading nerve tissue, such as herpes virus. I learned from him that yes indeed, his history of childhood illnesses included chicken pox, a member of the herpes family.

Returning home and no longer bound by my pledge, I reasoned that if his early exposure to a neurovirus, preconditioned his nerve cells to become super-sensitive (sensitized) to a subsequent neurologic insult (Cipro), then if true, possibly administration of immune globulin[2] (ig) might modify the effects of a theoretical virus component of the Cipro symptoms, at least temporarily. I learned that he has never received ig, but the whole notion of this approach led me into a new study on the use of ig in management of neurologic diseases, which I saw as possible support for this general thesis.

It turned out that there is a substantial body of work documenting the use of ig in several neurologic diseases, with results having one thing in common. Occasionally, while some problems respond to ig, nowhere could I find any explanation for the mechanism. It seems to me that if neurologic symptoms are ameliorated following ig, there is a reasonable chance that a neurovirus infection could have contributed to symptomology. I should point out that I hypothesized that my stroke symptoms seemed consistent with a diabetic-type neuropathy (book section Why Me?) and thus speculated that insulin resistance could be a factor in my case. I asked RG to watch for any effect on his symptoms following high sugar intake. He saw no effect. Turning this around, I cannot exclude a herpes effect on my stroke symptoms, since I have carried a latent herpes virus for as long as I can remember. About 20 percent of the population carries a latent herpes virus; it would be remarkable if such a possible relationship with stroke or other neurologic events has not reached mainstream thinking. I'll let someone else sort that out.

---

2   Immune globulin: a class of proteins produced in lymph tissue in vertebrates and that function as antibodies.

Why Interested in Immune Globulin

Immune globulin (ig) is essentially an encyclopedia of our health history involving our encounters with infectious agents. Immune globulin is the fraction of our blood that contains antibodies made throughout our life. We count on our reservoir of antibodies to meet, greet, and defeat any re-appearance of infectious agents previously encountered, to prevent a re-infection. We also count on antibodies produced from having been vaccinated, to prevent an initial infection from happening.

But here is news as quoted from an excellent review by M. C. Dalakas in 1997: "In controlled clinical trials, intravenous immune globulin (IVIg) has been effective in treating the Guillain-Barre syndrome,[3] multifocal motor neuropathy,[4] chronic inflammatory demyelinating polyneuropathy,[5] and dermatomyositis.[6] In other controlled or open-label trials and case reports, IVIg produced improvement in several patients with the Lambert-Eaton myasthenia syndrome[7] and myasthenia gravis[8] but had a variable, mild, or unsubstantiated benefit in some patients with inclusion-body myositis,[9] paraproteinemic IgM demyelinating polyneuropathy,[10] certain intractable childhood

---

3   Guillain-Barre syndrome is a disorder in which the body's immune system attacks part of the peripheral nervous system.
4   Multifocal motor neuropathy is a rare condition in which the muscles in the body become progressively weaker over months to years.
5   Chronic inflammatory demyelinating polyneuropathy (CIDP) is an acquired immune-mediated inflammatory disorder of the peripheral nervous system.
6   Dermatomyositis is a muscle disease characterized by inflammation and a skin rash. It is a type of inflammatory myopathy.
7   Eaton-Lambert syndrome, also called Lambert-Eaton myasthenic syndrome (LEMS), is a rare disorder affecting the muscles and nerves. LEMS is known to be associated with small-cell lung cancer. It may also be associated with cancers such as lymphoma or non-Hodgkin's.
8   Myasthenia gravis is an autoimmune neuromuscular disease characterized by recurring muscle weakness and fatigue.
9   Inclusion-body myositis (IBM) is an inflammatory muscle disease, characterized by slowly progressive weakness and wasting of both distal and proximal muscles.
10   Paraproteinemic IgM demyelinating polyneuropathy: chronic demyelinating polyneuropathy with benign IgM anti-myelin.

epilepsies,[11] polymyositis,[12] multiple sclerosis,[13] optic neuritis,[14] and the stiff-man syndrome."[15] Turning this around, if the etiology of any ig-ameliorated symptom is in question, then one avenue of study might include neuroviruses.

Guillain-Barre Syndrome (GBS)

An information sheet by Healthcommunities.com states that "the cause of GBS is not known; however, in about half of all cases **the onset of the syndrome follows a viral or bacterial infection, such as the following:** (Emphasis mine.)

- Campylobacteriosis (usually from eating undercooked poultry)
- Influenza
- Gastrointestinal viral infection
- HIV
- Infectious mononucleosis
- Porphyria (rare disease of red cells)
- Viral hepatitis"

Thus, with a record of these infectious agents associated with GBS, the stage is set for this disease to manifest when coupled with something like an autoimmune disease involving nerve tissue. Consistent with my hypothesis, we would expect symptoms to respond in some degree to immune globulin, even if it is first thought of as an autoimmune disease.

---

11   Childhood epilepsies: A recurrent disorder of the nervous system, character-ized by seizures of excessive brain activity which cause mental and physical dysfunc-tion, as convulsions, unconsciousness, etc.
12   Polymyositis is a relatively uncommon inflammatory disease that leads to significant muscle weakness.
13   Multiple sclerosis (MS) is a nervous system disease that affects the brain and spinal cord. It damages the myelin sheath, the material that surrounds and protects the nerve cells.
14   Optic neuritis is the inflammation of the optic nerve that may cause a com-plete or partial loss of vision.
15   Stiff-man syndrome: A chronic progressive disorder of uncertain etiology that is characterized by painful spasms and increasing stiffness of the muscles.

Just as with stroke, since influenza virus has also been implicated in GBS, one must wonder if vaccination for influenza or any of the other listed infectious agents has any impact on GBS incidence as it has with stroke. Sounds complicated, but may be worth a look. The big question would be whether the infectious agents preconditioned the nerve cells to become autoimmune-vulnerable, which seems like a clever and realistic possibility, or whether the autoimmune process preconditioned the body to be more vulnerable to infectious agents. I leave this to someone smarter than I am.

Puzzle pieces that seem to fit

An article appeared in a popular weekly magazine (Time Magazine, March 29, 2010) that described the experience of a female diabetic in her 50's who, after starting treatment with statin drugs for cholesterol management, soon experienced cognitive impairment. She observed that the problem resolved itself after she stopped the use of statins. I mention this as a possible practical life experience that seems to support my contention that a preexisting neurologic disease such as diabetes or possibly early Alzheimer's can precondition our bodies to respond in an exaggerated manner to a subsequent neurotoxic event such as use of a statin drug. This thought path would explain why not every person would develop neurologic symptoms following use of statins or perhaps to an antibiotic like Cipro. Those who develop neurologic symptoms likely have experienced previous recognized or unrecognized neurologic damage from a chemical, physical, or biological agent, according to my theory.

According to my hypothesis, this exaggerated statin effect easily could have been a case where a preexisting occult neuropathy (diabetic or even early Alzheimer's-related) was activated by a new neurologic insult in the form of a statin drug. This sounds a lot like the proposed type of mechanism associated with post-polio syndrome described above.

Additional Thoughts about This Hypothesis

The hypothesis predicts that any disease caused by an agent such as herpes virus that hides out in nerve tissue could become activated in the form of shingles, for example, if the body is subjected to a later neurological insult such as a stroke, or an encounter with a neurotoxic agent. In fact, there are numerous anecdotal reports of such re-activations. Also as mentioned, there seems to be reasonable possibility that a stroke event could uncover a latent neurologic genetic disease such as myotonic dystrophy or a diabetic-type neuropathy, as noted in the insulin resistance section.

From study of myotonia congenita, the impact of dietary sugar is described in a publication called *Jan's Diet for Myotonia*, where the author states that "even one gram of sugar in a slice of bread is enough to cause my [muscle] stiffness to increase", and notes that high glycemic foods, or anything that drives insulin higher, exacerbates symptoms of myotonia.

This phenomenon is consistent with my own observations regarding sugar aggravation of neuropathy in the stroke-affected side of my body. Thus, in my case, not only do I contend with what appears to be enhanced stroke-revealed insulin resistance-associated neuropathy, but also with what seems to be stroke-revealed elevated sugar sensitivity, as reflected by myotonia symptoms—a double whammy that so far has not cast a total debilitating effect, fortunately.

Chemotaxis

I have recklessly accepted the standard conundrum that the location of a stroke lesion is a random event driven by a 50-50 chance of which side of the brain will be affected. I now believe that is probably wrong in terms of clot-induced strokes, but probably true for spasm-induced strokes (TIAs). Let me first quote the definition of a word, and then I'll tell you why I raise the issue. Chemotaxis[16] is the phenomenon in which bodily cells, bacteria, and other single-cell or multicellular

---

16   *Chemotaxis*: any cell motion that is affected by a chemical gradient in a way that results in net propagation of a chemo attractant.

organisms direct their movements according to certain chemicals in their environment.

Recalling the paths of my warning strokes and my for-real stroke, it is way past coincidence that every event not only manifested on the left side of my body, but the residual effects on body parts were precisely the same with each event. Left leg, arm, hand, and shoulder compromised. Think about it: any of more than 100 billion neurons could have been hit. But stunningly, it appeared that the same neurons were hit on each separate occasion. If it were a matter of randomness, then surely at least one of the events would have affected the right side of my body, and the odds are staggering for multiple hits on the same neuron. So here is what I think should be considered.

Consistent with my hypothesis that an injured nerve becomes sensitized or "activated" so that any subsequent neurologic insult will re-activate the initial lesion, I judge this could be accomplished through the mechanism of chemotaxis.

According to the 2001 report by Bhalla, et al., "Patients with hyperglycemic cortical ischemia strokes *have higher neuron-specific enolase, an enzyme released from injured neurons,* (emphasis mine) compared with normoglycemic patients." This could, in theory, be the chemotactic agent needed to satisfy this hypothesis.

Why this type of event should direct new or repeat neurologic challenges toward the damaged neurons for body benefit is beyond my pay scale.

The Vitamin B Complex Dilemma

My neuropathy hypothesis, while obviously untested, nevertheless offers a plausible explanation for how and why neuropathies manifest. Until this book is published and experts can support or refute my contention, I feel an obligation to at least point out other implications, leaving it to the health-conscious readers to decide if what I say makes sense to them as they manage their health.

I believe that any damaged peripheral nerve becomes sensitized to future neurotoxic events, reacting with exaggerated response. It is important to notice that this predicts that subjects with diabetes, muscular nerve diseases, and the like could find that taking high doses of some of the B vitamins could be more harmful than helpful. But keep in mind that there is a peculiar property of some vitamin Bs, in that a deficiency can manifest as neuropathy, but so too can an excess manifest as a neuropathy—thus, the dilemma. To push into this problem just a little further, it is informative to also notice that the half-life of B6, for example, apparently can range from fifteen to twenty-five days, and for B12, its half-life in plasma is about six days, while its half-life in the liver is about twelve months, according to Adams (1963).

I am not an expert on vitamins, so this discussion is included only to alert the reader to the potential problem of consuming excess levels of B vitamins in an effort to manage your health. Naturally, you should discuss this point of view with your doctor.

Blood Sugar-Stress Relationship

Given the role of stress in stroke etiology, a fascinating theoretical sidebar to the story is the revelation by Rolef Ben-Shahar (1998) that the presence of stress hormones is associated with increased blood sugar. This implies that all the battles waged to manage blood sugar could be defeated by the presence of excess stress hormones. Beyond that scene, there is also the implication that we might not necessarily be able to totally blame insulin resistance/diabetes for "diabetic neuropathy," since long-term high stress alone could contribute to high blood sugar, which if high enough could translate into neuropathy.

Cortisol Neurotoxicity

It was a matter of hours before I planned to submit this manuscript to the publisher, when I awoke on the morning of April 26, 2011, with the idea that I had never checked the literature to find out if the stress hormone cortisol might be neurotoxic enough to delay the neurogenesis needed for my own recovery. Synchronicity to the rescue!

It turns out there is a wealth of information on this subject, found by Googling – cortisol neurotoxicity. Given the exceptionally high sense of stress in the four-year writing and completion process of this book I now have high hopes that my cortisol level will significantly decline and put me on the track for hypothyroid control and recovery from peripheral neuropathies.

While there are numerous gaps to fill in before arriving at the final word, I nevertheless offer this observation for the benefit of those who are faced with a parallel health issue and are looking for hope. No promises, but even a maybe, is better than no hope. Here is a quote from a product of the Brewer Science Library called New Horizons. "Excessive levels of cortisol are so detrimental to the brain and immune system that cortisol has been deemed by some as the "death hormone"." In this report, the author offers a list of nutrients that help reduce stress. This reference may be found under the title: Optimizing Brain Functions Part I: 21st Century Supplementation for slowing Neurological Deterioration & Maximizing Potential.

http:// www.mwt.net/~drbrewer/brainfunction 1.htm
Recovered on 4/26/2011

Intuition Trumps Data

In the book *MIND POWER into the 21st Century* by Kehoe (1987), a number-one world bestseller, the author notes the paths of numerous historic figures who attributed success to their trust in intuition. His examples include Mozart, Socrates, Einstein, Edison, Marconi, Henry Ford, Luther Burbank, Madame Curie, and "Nobel Laureates by the bundle" who have attributed their success directly to their intuition. He goes on to quote Henry Mintzberg from the *Harvard Review*, regarding a study of high-ranking corporate executives who were "constantly relying on hunches to cope with problems too complex for rational thinking". He concluded, ***"Success does not lie in that narrow-minded concept called rationality, it lies in a blend of clear headed logic and powerful intuition"***. (Emphasis mine.)

As a final notation, if this hypothesis is proven correct, the definition of insulin resistance as related to HBA1C will need drastic revision, probably reducing the range of normal to the Bernstein values (A1C 4.2-4.6) (2007). Also, if correct, we should immediately start tracking A1C values from early childhood to harvest time for the Grim Reaper. We urgently need to know what level of sugar consumption (A1C) becomes lethal.

A quick survey of A1C values among subjects with childhood obesity (CO) could put us on a path towards resolution of this problem. The caveat however, is that I believe we need to recognize a new standard normal value for A1C, set at a maximum of 5 percent, which then may make insulin resistance a strong predictor of CO.

CHAPTER FIVE

The Evolution Of Vascular Disease Study In America

Vascular disease management in America was brought into account around 1948, largely financed by the newly formed National Institutes of Health (NIH) in Bethesda, Maryland. This project was named the Framingham Study. Reporting from the book of Campbell and Campbell called The China Study; the fifty-year Framingham study has yielded more than 1000 scientific reports. Thinking about this in a cold harsh light, one would think that after 50 years of study if they were on the right track, we would have seen some favorable impact on stroke and heart attack statistics. While they have found that obesity, exercise, and smoking must be factored into health management, the fact remains that stroke and heart attack are still secure within the top three killer lists.

From what I can see some of the cherished findings of this work such as **elevated cholesterol, elevated blood pressure** and **atrial fibrillation** defy statistical efforts to indict them as causative. What seems to have happened is that these three risk factors became objects of study of how to mask the symptom with little regard for understanding the true root of the problem. This turned out to be a gift to the pharmaceutical firms, which encouraged them to produce even more drugs designed to conceal the symptoms without threatening the disease itself.

As an outsider, my comments may be subject to early dismissal, but I think a case can be made that for each of these "big three" symptoms, evidence is accumulating that inflammatory processes can be found under the symptoms. The schematic shown in this account of proposed mechanisms could easily be modified to picture how the inflammatory agents could apply not just to a fib, but possibly to BP and cholesterol risks as well.

I know it is dangerous and foolish to state the potential of one's own work. Sometimes intuition trumps science, and enthusiasm can be mistaken for fact. There would be nothing lost if we redirected some of our science resources from a search for symptom control to a search for disease prevention.

PART TWO

A Stroke Was My Teacher
LESSONS

INTRODUCTION TO LESSONS

The Experience of Stroke

Since I have used Part One of the book (Chapters) to describe the technical aspect of my embolic stroke experience, I must now summarize what it is I think I have learned in Part Two (Lessons).

First, I found out (IFO) that Einstein sure had it right when he observed that "Foolish faith in authority is the worst enemy of truth."

IFO that to make a significant and timely change in thinking, you must be prepared to "jump to conclusions" when your intuition tells you to do so (Lesson 7: The Intuitive Side of Stroke).

IFO that excess sugar consumption is a disease ticket, and evidence of its destructive impact was seen thirty years before I had any clue I was headed for a stroke. I had surgery for Dupuytren's contracture in the mid-1980s, which is now known to be a sign of high blood sugar, according to Bernstein. Remember Ronald Reagan and his love of jelly beans? Yes, he had Dupuytren's and made his exit also carrying the likely sugar burden of Alzheimer's. Many men also experience Peyronie's disease and carpal tunnel in their prime of life, which is similar to Dupuytren's contracture, as another sign of high blood sugar. Adding to that story, frequent fungal foot infections are common in diabetics, so alert physicians can help head off those possibilities if they take the time to factor in those signs and interpret A1C blood values properly. I will bet a chocolate-chip cookie that tennis elbow also has a sugar component to its etiology. The seemingly innocent link between Dupuytrens and diabetes cited by Bernstein, and the seemingly innocent link between Dupuytrens and iodine deficiency cited by Brownstein (shown on page 197 with Brownstein's permission)—implies that we should take a careful look to see if iodine deficiency contributes to diabetes.

IFO that excess sugar early in life can, in theory, set the stage for any number of neurologic events such as stroke, MS, and probably Alzheimer's—especially in those who are genetically predisposed.

Finally, IFO that it takes thick skin to resist the criticism of "authorities" who hold only traditional ideas yet are willing to denigrate anyone who tries to offer new, practical solutions to intractable problems. This type of response is what we have now come to expect.

Best advice? Follow Einstein's quote.

Why Me?

I guess it is natural to wonder how and why my body was positioned to experience a stroke. I can easily look back at my dietary habits and find leaks that could have led to a stroke (I guess). I think of the evil people who make candy bars that must have a secret ingredient known to corrupt good intentions. So I accept the lumps that must be taken for such indulgences—however, by and large, I took exceptional care of my body.

Back to the "why me" question—there is probably a genetic component in our family, in that four of the eleven children had some sort of stroke issue. Nonetheless, I look upon this experience as an opportunity to use my background as a lifelong scientist (thirty-seven years with Pfizer research and NIH) to construct this book in order to give hope and reality to anyone who experiences a stroke, and probably a heart attack too, since they are closely related, from my perspective. Yes, I embrace my predicament and am so thankful that it is not worse; I can speak, swallow, manage in and out of bed, as well as personal hygiene, and walk without assistance. I have typed this entire manuscript on a word processor with lots of word checks along the way. I can read and write and hopefully make a contribution to health management. Sure, things could still get worse; sure, I could croak at any time, and sure, the tennis and golf worlds will have a hell of a time getting along without me.

Speaking of golf, let me tell you a true story few golfers have ever experienced. I'm about fifty yards from the green (probably lying three), I take a full swing with my sand wedge, and the ball pops straight up in the air and lands in the divot, then the flap of sod falls over my ball. Oh well, another lost ball in the fairway. Not to worry, I've never threatened par golf and seldom even bogey golf. If anyone can tell me why an otherwise reasonably balanced guy would go to the golf course year after year to maybe hit one good shot out of a hundred swings, let me know. I think it must be some form of insecurity or insanity. It is like someone said—you keep making the same mistakes over and over again thinking you will get a different result sometime. (Einstein?)

Now, tennis was a little better. I remember one game where I served four consecutive aces to win a doubles match. I have always thought of tennis, golf, and bridge in the same light: the next round will surely be better. Back in my college days, I did have an opening seven no-trump bridge hand that I made. I doubt I shall ever be able to improve on that.

Stroke, It Is All in Your Head—or Is It

Most of us understand that stroke begins in the brain—earning the moniker "brain attack." But wait a minute, if it is the brain where damage is localized, what about the symptoms that affect the extremities? I'm talking about the symptoms such as sensation of swelling, the redness, the itching, numbness, burning, and everything called peripheral neuropathy. It seems quite clear that when something like sugar is consumed and your stroke-affected body parts immediately react as if the peripheral nerves are feeling a neurotoxin, then it can certainly create the impression that damage has occurred to peripheral nerves as well as to the brain. We attribute neuronal loss in the brain to clot-blocked oxygen and nutrients. So what is the mechanism for damage and damage control in peripheral nerves? I do not pretend to be a student of neurologic processes, so what I am asking may be old hat and well known to experts in that field, but as far as I can discern, the mechanism is not common knowledge. Here is some speculation which may at least raise some useful questions.

1. Why is it that many post-stroke peripheral neurologic symptoms seem to be precisely the same as those for diabetes, with the exception that stroke symptoms will be confined

to the stroke-affected side of the body, while with diabetes, both sides of the body can be affected?

2. Why do drug-related neuropathies such as those associated with statins, or with an antibiotic such as Cipro, also seem to pattern themselves somewhat similarly to the effects of diabetes or stroke? What is going on? By the way, if you want to know more about the side effects of statin drugs, Duane Graveline (2004) in his book, *Statin Drugs Side Effects,* covers the subject effectively.

3. Is it possible that once a nerve path is damaged by whatever means, those nerves will become super-sensitive to any future insult and then repeatedly display the same neurologic symptoms associated with the original sin whenever exposed to any neurotoxin? Whatever the case, the web of stroke effects is certainly not confined to the head, as our symptoms seem to reflect even remote nerve damage well beyond the damaged brain. Along this line, a patient with multiple sclerosis reported to me that sugar consumption is an issue for her as well. It is my impression, but I do not know for sure if that is a general observation among all MS subjects. I shall try to find out. Of course, it would be of great interest to test the same question among patients with all neurologic diseases. I do believe it pertains to Alzheimer's disease, for a starter. This line of thought has been discussed in the first part of the book called Neuropathy Hypothesis.

Closing the Loop

Here is what I think offers a reasonable explanation for the cause of my stroke. Retracing my own history leading up to embolic stroke, it seems plausible that my first encounter with the path happened as a teenager with a penchant for sweets, working in a candy store. This quite reasonably led to undiagnosed insulin resistance as an adult, with a resulting magnesium deficiency, which manifested as arrhythmia. The magnesium deficit, coupled with the likelihood of dehydration at that time, opened the door for red-cell and platelet agglomeration, followed by subsequent clot migration to the brain, resulting brain damage as shown in the flowchart (Chapter 3). It should be noted that the only non-prescription agent that proved useful without doubt, to control my arrhythmia, was a combination caplet of calcium, magnesium, and potassium. This was found several years ago in an anecdotal report about arrhythmia posted on the Internet. This issue was addressed by my use of additional calcium, magnesium, potassium—or more likely as I now view the issue, probably just magnesium alone. This becomes evident if I neglect to take magnesium, as arrhythmia usually resurfaces within a few days—I'm convinced, anyway.

I see three key questions which, if answered, might provide additional light to understand TIA and stroke:

1. Can a concomitant disease such as diabetes or even pre-diabetes (insulin resistance) make stroke or any other neurologic disease symptoms worse?

2. Can a concomitant disease such as stroke make diabetes symptoms worse?

3. Is it possible that the factor that determines whether one will manifest TIA symptoms or manifest full-blown stroke symptoms could be related to an underlying metabolic syndrome or some of those components?

The evidence that gives suggestive support to this notion is found in an observational study by Coutts, et al. (2005). Of 143 patients who had either a transient ischemic attack or a minor stroke, tracked by MRI scan, it was found that after thirty days post-event, 9.8 percent of these patients had new areas of ischemic stroke. Half the patients with new strokes experienced new stroke symptoms, but half did not. *Those who tended to have new stroke symptoms were those with the higher glucose values or were known diabetics.* (Emphasis mine.)

Naturally, a much larger study would be needed for confidence in this possible relationship. But hey, NINDS (National Institute of

Neurological Disorders and Stroke), this could be a pivotal study to put our research money to work, if not yet considered.

Here are some literature discoveries I have recently made that seem to tie many pieces of my stroke-related symptoms together. I do not offer these observations as fact, only that they make sense to me. First, as I look back, most of my issues appear to be stress related and thus probably associated with the stress hormone cortisol. Here are some of the issues that have presented themselves over the past few years. Foremost, is chronic stress dating back to my working days, followed by retirement and then exacerbated by the process of recording my stroke experience. This was never clinically measured, only symptomatically observed. These changes included some aspects of my post-stroke peripheral neuropathy that resembled diabetic neuropathy, as well as frequent urination, elevated cholesterol (300), and my version of insulin resistance (5.7) discussed and defended in the text.

Also observed was chronic constipation, and most of the symptoms associated with low thyroid. I want to emphasize that all of these thoughts are offered mostly for anyone who is trying to help manage their own health and who can relate to what I have described. In other words, consider this information only if it makes sense to you as a starting place for you to fill in gaps in your own health strategy. Beyond death and taxes, I am certain of nothing.

One of the best summaries I have come across dealing with the effects of cortisol can be found in an internet publication called *Back to Life Natural Health Center*. I recovered this document on 3-23-10 at http://www.backtolifehealth.com/Stress%20Detail.htm. The author was not identified.

Here are supplements I have come across and use, that are advertised as helpful for cortisol reduction. Be sure to get your doctor's advice before relying on this approach. They are:

- acetyl carnitine
- phosphatidyl serine – may be all one word
- alpha lipoic acid
- flavored Nordic cod liver oil

The most certain approach is to identify the stressing source and then eliminate it if possible. Simple to say; tough to do.

Effects of Excess Cortisol

The dominating effects of excess cortisol are pervasive and profound. Here are a few examples I have encountered:

A) In terms of neuropathy, excess cortisol is well documented as neuron-lethal. This is an immediate block to recovery from any neurologic disease where regeneration of nerve tissue is the goal.

B) In terms of hypothyroidism, excess cortisol inhibits conversion of T4 to T3, a vital step in thyroid function.

C) In terms of inconvenience, excess cortisol has been associated with constipation, as well as excess production of sebum (oily skin) and by inference, earwax. This subject area is easily accessed from internet studies.

D) Folded into the cortisol story is perhaps one of the most inconvenient features of my stroke experience. It turns out as I only recently discovered; peripheral neuropathy has been associated with hypothyroidism, so if the reader can identify with this issue, this is an angle to consider in health management.

Simple Truths About Stroke And Our Bodies

At the two-year anniversary of my stroke, I came to realize the need for an important change in mindset. During the initial two years, I focused my attention on seeking treatment modalities that might accelerate my recovery progress, as gleaned from Internet stroke literature. The reality, however, turned out to be that after two years of study, there was absolutely nothing I could point to with confidence that could be considered helpful in relieving symptoms or in accelerating recovery.

The one possible minor exception was the use of vibration, discussed under the Modalities Evaluated topic heading. In any event, the change in mindset was the insight that given the lack of any prospect of disease modification, I must instead focus on preserving, if possible, whatever level of functionality I still had.

It turned out that without realizing it, I actually had enviable mobility of the affected side of my body post-stroke, which I did not appreciate until I made a careful assessment of my capabilities, recalling them from the time immediately post-stroke, and comparing them with my status at the two-year anniversary mark. Using this test, I judged that strength and functionality of both the left hand/arm and the left foot/leg were noticeably less capable at the two- and three-year marks than immediately post-stroke—bummer.

I attributed this reality to the progressive loss of muscle mass that occurred over time. This observation was brought into focus when I recalled the words of a physiatrist, a rehabilitation physician specialist, early in the post-stroke days. She had counseled me that without good innervation and blood supply, it is impossible to build or rebuild muscle mass. While I was interested to be forewarned of this outcome, a strong part of my psyche rejected that thought, and I became all the more determined to strengthen my body through exercise. While I did recover the capacity to do push-ups to the level of 130 and jogged two miles on my eightieth birthday—two years post-stroke, there was still no escaping the fact that I had lost a good deal of body strength, which made me realize I needed to pay more attention to preserving what I still have than to looking for a magical recovery program.

In summary, while I can respect the wisdom of the physiatrist, I do not have to agree with her. As a stroke victim, you **must** drive yourself, both physically and mentally. Any level of functionality you can preserve will be the product of your effort alone; certainly no one else can do it for you. You can take this simple truth to the bank.

As we age, among other inconveniences, most of us will probably confront constipation, which also can be associated with stroke. While consuming extra water is crucial for many reasons, in my experience, it alone is not a reliable remedy. Since this conversation is significant to those with stroke, it may be helpful to review what seems to be useful and what does not. In pre-stroke years, I evaluated numerous strategies. I found that psyllium was indeed helpful for several months, but like so many other agents, it lost its utility over time. Similarly, most of the recognized laxatives had a short or non-existent useful life. In pre-stroke years, the only strategy that worked with lasting and predictable effect was a vegetarian diet.

One post-stroke strategy: a work in progress that seems to be helpful is to evaluate magnesium citrate in a liquid form. This is available at Wal-Mart at about a dollar a bottle, and is often the agent suggested when preparing for a colonoscopy. Here is what I found: if you consume about half to two-thirds of a ten-ounce bottle in a full glass of water according to the frequency of relief desired, you'll be smiling. Also, it is much cheaper than a dry product called Calm, which also is magnesium citrate-based but in a dry form. You might want to check it out anyway.

This material is said not to be habit-forming, as it relies on osmosis for drawing water into the bowel.

As alluded to previously, some stroke symptoms that seem to have abated after the first year of stroke in fact arose again inexplicably. For example, as time went by post-stroke, while moving around the house, it became necessary to rely on fixed objects for support after few steps, rarely walking directly to my goal. The left arm insisted on assuming a position across my abdomen with fist clenched; a rather common stroke effect, I found out. While that feature gradually reverted to a more normal posture, along with improved walking capability, nonetheless at the two-year mark post-stroke, I noticed a renewed attempt by my body to revert to the initial compromised pattern of post-stroke, thus requiring constant attention to overcome once more.

The point here is not to introduce a fear factor into the recovery process but rather to provide a heads-up on the surprise turns that can occur on the path toward recovery. It is a reality check for the unsuspecting. Hopefully, this will calm the concern of those who may endure a similar experience.

Another feature of post-stroke life, which only at the thirty-month mark did I begin to notice, was what Jill Bolte Taylor referred to in her book, *My Stroke of Insight,* as a sensitivity to the energy fields of those around you. Now, I do not know if this feature is common to all stroke victims, but I can say with confidence that for me, clearly I am increasingly sensitive to both the positive and negative influences around me.

In another part of this book I describe what I call "Truth in a Tuning Fork", which suggests a mechanism for explaining our relationships with other sentient beings in terms of resonance or dissonance. If this is indeed a product of stroke, it will need more practical documentation for confidence of reality. Whatever it is, it seems to me as potentially life-changing—stay tuned.

What our bodies can tell us

1. We know from ancient literature that weather has long been aliment associated. That weather conditions play into neurologic diseases was brought to my attention by my sister Carolyn Wernimont of Mt. Dora, Florida. After I reviewed how such things as high sugar consumption or high stress could be associated with my increased neurologic symptoms, she related how her late husband Ken Wernimont who carried a Parkinson's burden, often observed that weather changes had a strong effect on his symptoms. This story prompted me to look at published literature to see what has been written on the subject. I found evidence that cold weather is often associated with increased symptoms. Hot or cold weather can be a factor with multiple sclerosis subjects. Weather effects on muscular dystrophy and ALS has been reported. Peer reviewed weather documentation is beyond the intent for this book, but is mentioned for general interest for those affected.

2. Here is another body clue. I found that excessively oily skin (and probably excessive earwax) is associated with elevated stress hormone such as cortisol.

3. As for body weight management, associated with my intent to lower blood sugar as measured by the A1C test that within that effort, my job became one of trying to maintain body weight. Reducing sugar resulted in unwanted weight loss because my body was using fat and muscle protein to satisfy energy needs. The message is that in my opinion, you can dismiss all of the popular diet fads and accomplish even dramatic weight loss simply by removing all sugar and high glycemic foods from your menu. Your excess fat will melt away like lard in a frying pan, and here is why; simple sugars are the easiest energy source for our bodies to access. Take away the easy energy and your body will need, and it will rely on stored fat for energy.

4. Problems with elimination? While bran and other fiber foods are the usual remedy, you will find that a simultaneous high sugar intake will cancel any benefit from fiber.

5. The HBA1C problem once more. If you are trying to manage your own health choices and think what I say makes sense, then you had better become an authority on your blood sugar as measured by the HBA1C test. This was discussed previously at length in this book. It is so important; I must restate the problem and solution. There are only scattered reports that recognize that the true normal test value is 4.2-4.6 (Bernstein), or from my experience, certainly not over 5 percent. Most authorities (Einstein quote again) accept values as high as 7 percent as normal. With this high value for normal, we are exposing our children to excessive blood sugar levels that will lead to diabetes and certainly obesity and other neurologic diseases. Okay Mom and Dad – here is your assignment: start by asking your doctor to check the A1C level in your children. If it is over 5 percent, take the responsibility to remove sugar and high glycemic foods from the stuff your kids eat. How I wish I had this advice in my youth. Take this path and watch childhood obesity and other problems disappear.

The Brain Game—Mostly Losers

Since this book is meant to offer solution for neurologic and vascular diseases, the game plan deserves a review so that the readers can decide for themselves, what makes sense.

When one thinks about how remarkably adept our bodies are in self-repair, within our game plan for health strategy, must be provisions for allowing self-repair to proceed without challenge or interruption. Think about this: neuroplasticity/neurogenesis, the ability of our bodies to provide new nerve pathways for damaged nerves has been described previously in this book as my major source of hope for stroke recovery.

But wait a moment please, while patience is required for nerve regrowth, we must be certain we are not interfering with the process by ingesting neurotoxic foods like sugar, elevated insulin, or nutrients like excesses of selected B vitamins, or drugs that themselves are suspects as being neurotoxic such as, statins, Coumadin, or any other drug with no public record of its neurotoxic status. For unsuspecting subjects with a disease such as MS, MD, ALS, Diabetes, Parkinson's, Alzheimer's, Stroke, or any of a litany of other possibilities, their first goal must be to have confidence that whatever they put into their bodies is not doing more harm than good. This is a tough nut to crack in our symptom focused health society, as maybe no one knows for sure what helps and what hurts.

Let me put this a little stronger: In my opinion, there is no way on God's green earth that anyone can hope to recover from any neurologic disease, if within their treatment regimen they are ingesting substances that are simultaneously destroying the new nerve tissue that allows neuroplasticity to occur. Look at the history of MS or MD, as two obvious examples of the problem. Throw in Parkinson's and stroke, and measure the paltry progress made in the last 25 years or more. Tons of money thrown at the problems, micrograms of progress. When you stop to think about it – to be almost cruel but realistic, where is the incentive for our health guides to solve any problem that will result in loss of income for their industry? No matter how you answer this question, it still does not explain why government laboratories seem to be in bed with the businesses they regulate.

So what can we do to overcome the inertia? Here is what I think must happen. Reread Chapter Four - Puzzle Piece that Seem to Fit. Use the example cited and take the responsibility for observing your own change in symptoms that you associate with the use of a prescription or supplement. Obviously, it is going to be up to the public to tell their health care guides about any changes they observe. The reality is that neither the doctors nor the pharmaceutical firms have any incentive to reveal any risks not required unless there is a financial advantage. In short, medical services as currently structured are not working, and never will until we start rewarding the health industry for prevention rather than for symptom management.

Who Dunit?

Here is one of the sometimes-fascinating sideshows between me, myself, and I, that go on in those of us who are fascinated with mind games. Nearly finished with this book. I finally got around to ask myself if diabetic neuropathy is really a direct product of high blood sugar, or might it be equally possible that high insulin itself is neurotoxic.

To answer that question, a literature search on April 7, 2011, yielded a report by Noh, Lee, Ahn, Hong, and Koh. In their 1999 report they observed that their result "suggests that insulin can be both neuroprotective and neurotoxic in the same cell system but by ways of different signaling cascades". They found in mouse cortical cultures, insulin induced neuronal necrosis within 48 hours of exposure. Whether this translates to animal response was not discussed.

Alternatively, is this search path that came to me: Glucose neurotoxicity as discussed by Tomlinson and Gardiner (2008), state "Neurons have a high glucose demand and unlike muscle cells they cannot accommodate uptake under the influence of insulin. Neuronal glucose uptake depends on the extracellular concentration of glucose, and cellular damage can ensue after persistent episodes of hyperglycemia—a phenomenon referred to as glucose neurotoxicity. This article reviews the pathophysiological manifestations of raised glucose in neurons and how this can explain the major components of diabetic neuropathy."

Treatment Modalities Evaluated

I have given frank assessments of several treatment modalities. If you think I have been harshly critical of some of them, you would be right. However, if you look objectively, you may at least save yourself the time, the money, and the hope lost while walking those paths.

My search will continue for the balance of my life. With a little luck, maybe the stroke-management industry can adjust their vision of how stroke victims should be managed.

Of course, maybe my views will also need to change before the ninth inning is over.

STANDARD MODALITIES

Occupational Therapy

Not assessed.

Physical Therapy

Physical therapy (PT) or occupational therapy is really the only treatment modality consistently recommended for stroke rehabilitation. As I worked my way through two services, one in 2007 and one in 2009, I noticed some consistency in approach, which for both included exercise routines to address flexibility, strengthening, endurance, balance, and posture. My problem with PT was convincing myself that

PT could actually lead me to a level of recovery that my body could not accomplish with time alone.

For the skeptic, since the majority of healing seems to occur in the first three months post-stroke, one test of validity of physical therapy rests with two questions: Did the first three months post-stroke provide the platform for natural healing to occur independent of PT? Or did PT provide the platform for the majority of natural healing to occur in the first three months post-stroke?

Common sense tells me this is an unanswerable question, and that we should use all tools available during recovery, regardless of proof.

However, given the extensive history and practice of physical therapy, I concluded that the success of physical or occupational therapy becomes a statistical exercise comparing long-term outlook and quality of life with those who had and those who did not have PT. In that light, PT is easily justified and recommended, as I read the literature.

While the path to stroke recovery usually takes the patient through some version of physical therapy, in my opinion, the strategies used by therapists seemed to depend more on what equipment was available in their facility than on a program driven by a protocol proven to be effective. We do recognize that every patient is unique and no one shoe fits all—thus, by necessity, PT must be tailored for each patient. While that seems entirely reasonable, it still appears to me that a facility must be certified to perform physical therapy that meets Medicare, insurance, and common-sense standards, and that there must be defined equipment available and staff training that meet accepted qualifications. So where does one find documentation of standards for physical therapy facilities? I looked but got lost in the maze of Medicare regulations. I defy anyone to find what they are looking for, as Medicare regulations clearly were designed for job security, not for easily accessible documents.

For my second therapy session, I quickly found that there was big trouble ahead for any self-proclaimed macho man who insisted on doing twenty reps when asked to do ten, or double or triple the exercise plan recommended. Take my word for it: this is the *wrong* thing to do. It is highly counterproductive. In any event, I found that the therapist, in her gentle way, could easily extract a cry of "uncle" from me whenever

I got out of hand, and I learned not to mess with her instructions. One of her most illuminating and motivating observations was as follows: "Stroke recovery is a supply-and-demand proposition."

As many of those recovering from stroke may know, there have been numerous television programs, mainly on PBS, that document the ability of the brain to compensate for loss of neuronal function by what is termed *plasticity*. Plasticity refers to the formation of new compensating neuronal pathways which form, regardless of age, after focal brain damage has occurred. In practice, this is what each of us must count on, with certain caveats for any hope or prospect of regaining lost body function, and indeed recovery has been reported even after many years post-stroke. As a case example, for Jill Bolte Taylor (2009), the neuroanatomist, who wrote the highly acclaimed book, *My Stroke of Insight,* it was eight years after her massive hemorrhagic stroke that she regained use of the affected side of her body, enabling her to resume teaching. Thus, the question arises as to whether there is anything that anyone can do to help accelerate the neuroplastic process. Within that context, I fall back to the advice of my therapist, where she noted that neuroplasticity is best observed when the body sends an unambiguous message to the brain that help is wanted and needed. This message is most effectively transmitted when the affected body part resumes its responsibility to at least try to perform the tasks it did pre-stroke.

If the left side of the body, for example, cedes its job to the right side of the body, then the brain never receives a clear message that the left side needs an alternate nerve track, and the process of neuroplasticity will be left on the back burner. While this may come across as a simplistic interpretation of how the body works, I found the idea to be a powerful motivator and reminder to constantly challenge the compromised body function to try to do what it is supposed to do and not become satisfied letting the opposite side of the body do all the work. This is precisely what I finally came to realize as a critical contribution to the path to recovery. If you have left leg weakness, for example, you will find that the left leg will become perfectly happy to let the right leg take over, and you can enjoy a Herman Munster gait forever, as your right leg does its best to handle the walking function single-handedly, or should we say single-leggedly. My therapist also made her point quite clear when I arrived one morning for my PT session and she marched me to a full-length mirror and said, "Now look at yourself. Your right sleeve is neatly rolled up, but you have totally ignored your left arm sleeve"—translated to mean I had given up on my left arm as being of use. I sure did not realize what I was doing, and it never happened again, but I do often think about her object lesson. This was especially notable while typing with a left hand that preferred I rely on spell check rather than to make the extra effort to type correctly in the first place. I say that hand has a mind of its own and we are still not always on speaking terms. And by the way, I understand that it is possible to fool the brain in a helpful way by standing in front of a full mirror while doing PT. It seems that the image now appears to show the compromised left side, for example, now as perfectly functional.

The brain seems to fall for the ruse, allowing the subject to resume good terms with brain function. I am sure the reader can find a complete description of this strategy by doing an Internet search using terms that include *physical therapy* and *mirror*. I am currently evaluating the idea.

What caused me to challenge how PT is administered rests with the fact that after my stroke, I was directed by my primary care physician to use a local service. As time went by, I came to realize that particular physical therapy service did not have provisions for such things as hydrotherapy, electro stimulation, or vibration options. Exercise equipment was very limited as well, yet somehow they qualified as a physical therapy facility. It makes one wonder how in the world the unsuspecting is supposed to know how to distinguish a well-qualified service from a marginal service. Here is where an advocate—discussed later—would have been invaluable.

What was more disturbing was the fact that there were absolutely no objective measurements of muscle strength, proprioception (body awareness), gait status, or response to any other possible treatment options, as all records were products of subjective assessments by the staff, with no way to generate or record electronic data. This was also true for early assessment of stroke damage by attending neurological specialists, as it was only their judgment that reflected strength of grip or ability to follow a finger path, etc. It would be impossible for any subsequent doctor to make any valid comparison with the findings from the initial examination. Yet the assessment was paid for as something useful, and accepted even without electronically recorded data.

This experience was clearly an unnecessary medical expense relegated to the useless information file in terms of comparing my initial neurologic assessment with any subsequent neurologic assessment by the same or a different neurologist. My experience may not necessarily reflect the way health care is managed in larger metropolitan areas in the United States. But it sure does call into question why Medicare would be willing to pay anyone for a service without evidence from automatically recorded data to support the findings. This applies to every single service within our health care system, including rehab of all stripes—a subject discussed in Appendix IV, dealing with Medicare.

The extent of PT treatments (back to that subject) seems to be based upon some arbitrary time (apparently decided by Medicare), rather than status of recovery. In my judgment, the therapists obviously wanted to maintain their income stream, so they were happy to keep you engaged as long as possible. In my case, on more than one occasion, I withdrew after a few weeks of evaluating modalities, if I could not sense any benefit from the program. This was driven by my belief that Medicare was being ripped off. It struck me that it would be impossible to prove that PT can do more than what your body is capable of doing with time alone. About the same time I completed my first PT sessions, I visited a new neurologist for consultation. The first thing he asked was whether I was still receiving PT, and he went on to say, "Well, I can tell you that you will not receive further benefit if you are." This is not what I wanted to hear; I wanted some reason for hope of improvement—at least a suggested alternative. I totally rejected the implication that I would not get better with effort.

It should be noted that my stroke was characterized as mild, yet all in all, I concluded the success level of PT as I observed the practices hinges on expectations. Naturally, one can be easily disappointed if expectations are not proportional to reality. Since I did not know the reality of PT, I first concluded that the human body likely can take care of itself quite well and is much smarter than is credited. But do keep in mind that if had I experienced issues with speech, swallowing, communicating, personal care, or a litany of other possible stroke-related symptoms, my assessment of PT might have been entirely different. As long as no one important challenges the quality of health care in America, we will get what we deserve. I also noted that the reports of PT status sent to the prescribing physician seemed at times inflated. This was observed in every rehab service I attended. It struck me that the reports were designed more to ensure the prescribing doctor that their decision to recommend the service was appropriate and effective than to convey meaningful results. It probably did not matter, because *never* did the prescribing physician ask me for my assessment of the therapy. Translation: my guess is that they knew exactly what was going on and never read the reports anyway.

OTHER MODALITIES BRIEFLY EVALUATED FOR STROKE RECOVERY

In each evaluation, recommendation by the provider was to continue treatment for best results. However as a matter of out-of-pocket practicality, if I could not sense any prospect of progress, I usually limited my evaluation to three weeks.

Acupuncture

My conclusion, after sessions with two different therapists, is that if you picture the body in terms of a hologram, then every cell of the body contains the same information as the entire body, as referenced by Talbot (1991) in *The Holographic Universe*. Pictured in a chart (map) on the wall of the acupuncture treatment rooms are images of the ear or ear lobe, each depicting acupuncture sites said to influence various body organs. By placing needles at various strategic spots, one can "unblock" the energy force called chi, effecting a desired relief of pain or of that organ-associated ailment.

Returning to the scene in terms of a hologram where every cell of our body contains the total details of the entire body, then it follows that there should be no need to create explanatory energy channels or maps called meridians and place needles into those channels to achieve the so-called unblocking of chi. In fact, if there is substance to the notion, it should be possible to place needles anywhere in the body and receive the benefits propounded. It seems to me that the idea of a holographic universe should be folded into the early Chinese concepts. If one includes the thinking of Zukav (1997) in *The Dancing Wu Li Masters*; *The Field-The Quest for the Secret Force of the Universe* by McTaggart (2002); and most recently, *The Biology of Belief* by Lipton (2008), then a more comprehensible role of acupuncture begins to take shape. However, it seems to me that the key element still missing is that of intention as described by Dyer (2004) in *The Power of Intention*. I suspect there are aspects of acupuncture beyond those stated above, making it a useful adjunct to health management for reasons not defined. I, however, concluded that acupuncture, as practiced in my case, offered nothing substantive in terms of stroke recovery. However, I would keep an open mind for any practitioner of acupuncture who could provide certifiable evidence of effectiveness for embolic stroke recovery.

The notion that symptoms may be caused by chi blockage is hard to swallow when the therapist resorts to a pinched nerve or stressed muscle to explain the cause of chi blockage in the first place. A truly skilled therapist would likely refute this statement immediately.

Chiropractic

At about thirteen months post-stroke, I began an evaluation of chiropractic for stroke recovery. The process began like all other modalities I tested, with a series of questions for the therapist. My first question was about his experience in treating stroke, which I was assured that he had. Of course, like all other modalities, there was a (magical and predictable) 80 percent probability of success. I made it clear from the get-go, I was not interested in an X-ray assessment of my problem; thus, we began with a series of treatments to "align my vertebrae" using a mechanical treatment table where a trip of a lever would suddenly drop a portion of the body. I endured three treatments the first week, terminating the evaluation due to significant left shoulder/arm-stretch stress, which has persisted to date (forty months).

The only thing useful to come from this trial was the therapist's observation that while some leg muscles were weak, others were very strong. Although his counsel was for me to continue the treatment protocol, my assessment was that no amount of manipulation could possibly restore muscle functionality, since what I needed for that to happen was renewed nerve and blood supply—something I should have considered long before the chiropractic evaluation. I cannot certify that the shoulder issue that I associated with manipulation was solely due to chiropractic, since the shoulder in question was the side of my body that was stroke-affected. My suggestion if asked: forget chiropractic and move on. Again, it may not be fair to judge chiropractic on such limited experience.

Massage

Consistent with evaluation of other modalities, I first asked if massage has been used successfully in stroke management; I came away with a qualified yes, however there were no specific examples given. The therapist was optimistic that with sufficient treatments, massage could improve functionality of the stroke side of my body, or at least in her view, keep symptoms from getting any worse. This evaluation was done nine months post-stroke using one-hour sessions two to three times per week. The therapist did leg-, foot-, and shoulder-focused massage and also did reflexology on the foot, which at times seemed to hit "electric sensation" spots on the stroke foot that were not noted on the normal foot.

Immediately post-stroke, continuing to date forty months post-stroke, I complained of a sense of swelling in the groin area at the top of the arch where leg meets torso, as well as swelling in the foot and calf of the affected leg. She suggested that lymph may be accumulating and tried to massage the swelling away from the area. I thought this was a reasonable notion, so I continued the sessions for about six weeks.

Since I could not discern that my overall stroke status was improved, I discontinued the assessment. It is impossible to know whether massage would prevent symptoms from getting worse, since there is no way to run a control.

My overall evaluation of massage is that without documented proof of benefit, I would give it no more than a pleasant experience rating, and skip it for meaningful contribution to recovery. As noted later, I observed that a hand-held vibrator applied to the affected body side, seemed every bit as useful as the massage experience. (Both are said to induce endorphins.)[1]

As another side note about stroke effects, while my body tells me my hand is cold or my foot is swollen—it is odd but true that one hand is actually no colder than the other hand, as determined by my wife—they just feel that way to me.

Water Therapy

Not a fair trial, as water was much too cold—I stayed for one treatment of the dismal experience. Guess what? Medicare paid anyway for an aborted and totally useless "therapy". I described what happened to the prescribing physiatrist, but it was never acknowledged. Either Medicare does not know or they do not care. What a waste of health care funds! Without doubt—cost control for health care should begin with a Medicare overhaul. Our hospitals, therapists, and physicians may be getting a bum rap. (More on Medicare in Appendix IV.)

---

1   Endorphins: Any of several peptides secreted in the brain that have a pain-relieving effect like that of morphine.

ELECTRO STIMULATION

In a Physical Therapy Setting

Of no benefit whatever for my issues. Another example where the PT service was so poor, I had to tell the therapist that his stimulation device did not read the stimulation level he said it was set to deliver. Yup, Medicare got hooked for that useless exercise as well.

Using a TENS[2] Unit

Of no benefit whatsoever.

Using an Internet-Advertised Device Called Rebuilder

This was not an inexpensive full sixty-day trial. If anything, my symptoms were exacerbated. More harm than good, in my experience.

Vibration

Vibrating Platform (principle developed from Russian space studies) said to improve nerve transmission. I evaluated a machine called Zenergy Vibes. This model was around $300 through Target online. I used it eleven minutes daily for two months, with no certain indication of benefit. If a professional unit, as used in some NFL training rooms, were available, I would want to evaluate it.

Before dismissing this approach, I can update the assessment as follows: I found that at the forty-month mark post-stroke, numbness in the left foot and leg seemed more apparent. I re-evaluated the vibrating platform and this time got the impression that the symptoms abated with combining hand-held vibration with platform vibration.

I judged intuitively that subjects with profound foot numbness might want to evaluate this modality.

---

2   TENS Unit: Transcutaneous electrical nerve stimulation, small devices that ease chronic pain by blocking pain signals using electrical stimulation.

Hand-Held Vibrator

My Wal-Mart unit is probably the most useful tool found to help alleviate some of the symptoms of neuropathy. This device is especially helpful for massaging legs and arms for symptomatic relief. (Homedic, percussion massager with heat around $30.)

I found it surprisingly effective in moderating some of the neuropathies, such as numbness, swelling, itching, burning, and general discomfort.

EFT—Emotional Freedom Technique

This procedure was physician recommended. I suggest you Google it to get details. I was unable to determine any beneficial effect on stroke; however, it carries some high recommendation.

Hyperbaric Oxygen Treatment (HBOT)

By January of 2008, seventeen months post-stroke, I had invested considerable effort trying to understand what happens to the body following stroke and what is thought to cause post-stroke symptoms. The literature is consistent (as revealed by the Internet and various books) that stroke symptoms are a reflection of the portions of the brain where an infarct (nerve damage) has occurred, as a result of an embolic shower, in my case.

I came to realize that my brain was damaged and that damage was largely the result of oxygen/nutrient deprivation following blockage of blood supply. This was probably caused by clots/plaque debris that was released either from the heart itself or from vessels leading to the brain. I learned that tissue around damaged nerves is referred to as the *penumbra*, containing cells that are still alive. Though inactive, they still have the potential to "re-awaken" and support new blood supply and signal transmission pathways, to eventually re-establish new connections between the brain and the affected part(s) of the body. This is referred to as brain plasticity.

As I pondered this scenario, I reasoned that if penumbral areas were asleep due to oxygen deprivation, oxygen under pressure very well might be a way to push oxygen into those sleeping cells. With that reasoning, I started a search for what is known about stroke recovery using high-pressure oxygen treatment. It turned out that like most other (new) ideas, I was not the first to think of this approach. Within the wealth of information published along this line are numerous reports describing dramatic recoveries following devastating strokes, even many years after the event occurred. With this exciting possibility, I immediately began a search for an HBOT service in my area. I was referred to one just a few miles away called Mountain HBOT in Etowah, North Carolina.

This firm was created after an officer of the company was said to regain about 80 percent of function (after having suffered a shower of strokes two years prior). He bought his own chamber and now sells chamber time. This facility uses 100 percent oxygen, delivered at one and a half times atmospheric pressure for one-hour daily treatments. The treatment protocol may vary from one facility to another based on the issue being addressed. Some programs involve fifty to sixty treatments, none of which is recognized for payment for stroke-related issues by insurance companies or by Medicare at the time of this writing. This particular organization offered treatment payable on an hourly basis at the rate of $225 per sixty-minute treatment or for $200 per treatment with ten sessions paid up front, which was my plan. I have noticed other facilities in other states such as Florida that charge much less. In fact, some of the most informative publications on HBOT were by Neubauer at Lauderdale-by-the-Sea in Florida. There are numerous references to HBOT facilities that can be accessed through the Internet.

Several parameters need to be considered for HBOT sessions. One is concentration of oxygen (which in this case was 100 percent). The higher concentrations used are not necessarily more desirable, and in fact may be less preferred.

1. Oxygen pressure during treatment may vary with problem addressed perhaps ranging from 1.5 to 2.5 atm (atmospheres).

2. Treatment time.

3. Frequency and duration of each treatment.

4. Availability of physician on site during treatment—in my case, there was none. I believe this is an exception to the norm.

I started HBOT on January 7, 2008 and ended my sessions two days later on January 9. My rationale for discontinuing the program after three sessions is detailed as follows.

Session 1: Jan. 7, 2008

The chamber exposure was one hour, as planned. Upon exiting the chamber, I mentioned that the environment seemed very stuffy and too warm, and that I did not notice the cooling phase I was told to expect. There was a slight feeling of nausea, although I did not mention it at the time, since I did not know what is "normal" for the procedure.

It was not the refreshing experience followed by a sense of "well-being" I had read in the literature. It was more of an environment giving way to a feeling of oxygen deprivation, noticing I craved a breath of fresh air during the procedure.

Session 2: Jan. 8, 2008

Considering my response to the first session, I requested that this second session be forty-five minutes (which is not an unusual treatment time in some programs). This experience was more comfortable than the first. I did notice the cooling phase that I anticipated. I also noted in my log of the experience that I again felt a modest sense of nausea and lack of ability to get a deep breath of air.

Session 3: Jan. 9, 2008

From exposures to HBOT in sessions one and two, I had a growing sense of concern for the ability of my body to tolerate this process, and as a result, I requested termination of the third treatment after thirty-three minutes. This request was driven mostly by a bodily reaction more intense than previous (nausea), and included a disconcerting series of muscle spasms or twitching on the stroke-affected side of my body.

After these failed to subside, I sensed that I was receiving more oxygen than my body could tolerate and that I needed to stop further exposure. (From this experience, I judge that 100 percent oxygen could qualify as a neurotoxin for purposes of my neuropathy hypothesis.)

Upon returning home from my third treatment session, I checked the Internet to learn the symptoms of oxygen toxicity and found that nausea and muscle spasms are consistent with that syndrome. I should mention that in preparation for entering an HBOT program, I read several books and innumerable studies and found not one negative report for the procedure as applied to stroke management. Thus, I was totally unprepared for the possibility that my body might react atypically.

In defense of my decision to discontinue treatments, I doubt there is anyone who could have a more solid background for making an informed decision to evaluate HBOT for stroke management issues. There is no one who could have higher expectations for a beneficial outcome and be more convinced of its potential benefits. Similarly, I doubt there could be a stronger advocate for the procedure with a successful outcome. Thus, it was not as if I entered the program with nothing more than a wishful attitude. I have always been physically fit and have a long history of running and aerobic exercise, which may play into my body's response to pure oxygen.

I also noted in my log of the experience that my decision to terminate the treatment at this time did not preclude the possibility that I may choose to return for further treatments at a future date. I am fully convinced of the merits of HBOT, and if by chance I should have another stroke episode, I would want to return for treatment on an emergency basis, using a modified protocol. Indeed, in March of 2009, which was nineteen months post-stroke, since I had nothing that showed any sign of affecting my recovery path in a positive way, I requested an appointment to try HBOT again. The provider declined to accept me for further treatment, citing my previous adverse experience.

The decision whether to employ high-oxygen treatment is not without controversy, and to be fair, you may note the work of Bhalla, Wolfe, and Rudd (2001) where they state, "Evidence shows that stroke patients have lower oxygen saturation compared to matched controls." They go on to cite "with highly enriched oxygen, that increased mortality was observed in animal models". They also noted that mitochondrial respiration is impaired, and that hyperoxia induces cerebral vasoconstriction, which may reduce cerebral blood flow. They quote several reports where supplemental oxygen had no benefit on survival, and speculated that oxygen free radicals caused further tissue injury. They did suggest that further research is needed.

Given the gravity of stroke and heart attack, the notion that these purported negatives are consequential, fade to irrelevance, in my opinion. The measurement of hypoxia itself is not unchallenged, as I read the literature.

Having studied hundreds of stroke-related references in support of the book, I want to point out that the paper by Bahalla, Wolfe, and Rudd is among the most informative and useful. Anyone doing a serious stroke study will find the reference helpful.

My most urgent plea to stroke-management resources around the world is to please take a more careful look at HBOT, to see if there is a protocol design that can be documented as safe, reliable, and beneficial. Knowing it can work anecdotally, possibly all we need are more data defining the optimal conditions.

Esoteric Energy Healing

How does esoteric healing work? When a person is healthy, the energy field is evenly balanced in all the seven major energy centers of the body. Any imbalance in this energy ultimately manifests itself in the form of physical or mental ailments.

A therapist trained in **esoteric healing** learns how to identify the areas where the energy field is imbalanced by using his or her hands to scan the energy field of the patient.

This modality has inspired me to take up the study with determination. I have alluded to my experience several times in the text and am fully convinced of its merits. Having said this, after several sessions and deep pursuit of the concept, I have not been able to attain evidence of its utility for my stroke issues. I can say that complementary to esoteric healing, I noticed that the book *Quantum-Touch—The Power to Heal* by Richard Gordon offers a powerful adjunct strategy to esoteric healing. I continue to pursue both paths.

Craniosacral Massage Healing

The craniosacral massage involves the bones of the head, the spinal column, the sacrum, and the underlying structures. A craniosacral massage implies the use of hands. The hands gently touch the surfaces and add pressure to certain points through special techniques.

A limited exposure to craniosacral massage yielded only a very superficial evaluation, as my therapist suggested that I should focus more on tai chi for my stroke issues. My brief assessment is that I believe there is potential for this approach, but I did not evaluate it sufficiently to obtain evidence of utility.

Brain State Conditioning

The premise of Brain State Conditioning (BSC) is one that involves neurofeedback, where following placement of electrodes on the scalp, various classes of brain waves can be recorded. In this program, once your base line profile has been established, the treated subject watches a computer screen while various audio signals are supplied. The goal is for the subject to recognize when the brain waves lie in a "normal" range. Gradually your visual assessment learns to influence and change the brain wave pattern to a more desirable profile. This process has been used with some dramatic results for war zone traumatic brain damage, stuttering, and for numerous other issues such as Attention Deficit/ Hyperactivity Disorder, stress, sleep disorder, epilepsy, as well as chronic fatigue syndrome, fibromyalgia and many others. I see great potential for this adjunct to health management.

In my program, the treatments ran about one hour each for 12 sessions occurring about every other day. These were out of pocket costs not recognized by insurance at $100.00 per session. The sponsors of this program made no claim for stroke success, yet I chose to evaluate it for purposes of this book and from my physician recommendation. This occurred in January and February of 2008. The therapist offered this assessment. "In my opinion, the Brain State program did not work for Jim Crawford because his brain did not get to the point of receiving and utilizing information the BSC method provides. With additional training, we might see his brain listening and responding more consistently, but one Intensive (series of sessions I gather) had little lasting impact on Jim's energy signature.

In summary, no promise was made, and no benefit within my budget, was received. My conclusion: this was not a useful modality for my type of neurologic injury.

Health Maintenance Post-Stroke

No one can know the specific health pattern that leads to any stroke, beyond the accepted general list that includes high blood pressure, diabetes, and other conditions such as dehydration, unbalanced blood lipid profile, and inactivity as some of the main ones. It is equally unlikely anyone can know what to do beyond the remedy for those specific factors listed—to minimize their further stroke risk. While that is certainly true for me, I nevertheless offer my opinions of what I think makes sense for post-stroke health maintenance.

Health Maintenance Opinions

1. While it is not practical to carry an oxygen tank around, I think that if you have even a small emergency oxygen supply such as a Third Lung (less than $150.00), as used by mountain climbers, it might provide enough oxygen to get you to the hospital while in an oxygen crisis following a heart attack or stroke. At the very least, intuitively it seems to me that anyone who senses symptoms of stroke or heart attack might help him- or herself by immediately hyperventilating until help arrives—what's to lose?

2. Probably the single most powerful thing you can do to minimize the possibility of another stroke is to drink at least an extra two quarts of water per day, spread through the day. *Do not wait until you are thirsty to drink.* Drink even when you are not thirsty, since as we age, we do not have

reliable thirst signals, as discussed under the dehydration topic in Part 1. It is not easy to force yourself to drink extra water. Here is a suggestion: each time you use the lavatory or pass by a Brita jug on your desk, counter, etc., during your daily routine, use those events as a reminder to immediately drink some water. Read or reread the section on stroke mechanisms to get you pumped.

3. Do not fool yourself into thinking other liquids will do; they will not. Colas, coffee, and alcoholic beverages are actually dehydrating agents. ***Do not drink large volumes of water at any one time, as excess water can be toxic—even fatal*** (Benkim 2009).

4. One of the first things to do while recovering after having a stroke is to start a daily log or diary of your state of health. Make a video record of yourself in action during the course of your recovery—done on a monthly basis, I suggest—showing how you manage your daily routine. This is important, because although you think you can distinguish one day's details from another; changes are so gradual that it is impossible to point to a time when a change occurred. Within your diary, write down when you visit a doctor, especially a new one; make notation of the date of visit and a summary of the doctor's comments and recommendations. Since it did not occur to me to make a video record, I do not have one, but I have wished many times that I did. Why is this so important? Without it, you cannot know if any addition or deletion from your diet, such as a nutrient/supplement or medication, or even a new physical therapy experience, was related to your recovery path. In addition, you should try to rate your bodily functions monthly. Any physical or mental impairment should be graded on a scale of one to ten. You want to know if any activity can be related to your recovery status. No one can help you on this issue; it is up to you to do the science and bring any significant change to the attention of your doctor as you

think necessary. They will be better able to help you help yourself. Examples of impairment you may want to track would be such things as development of clonus,[1] foot drop,[2] general mobility, numbness, swelling, elimination issues, or changes in mental attitude/depression. Anything that you consider a limitation needs to be noted and recorded. You may be wondering what difference it makes if you keep this record or not, since there is precious little anyone can do about anything stroke-related, it seems. But not so fast! Your stroke has put you in a position to observe and possibly help with the understanding and management of this medical problem—that's the way I view it anyway—so I encourage you to make the effort.

5. Sweets are *not* treats—opt for the tricks. If you consume high-glycemic[3] foods such as sugars of any variety to the point that you crave them, I predict you have already crossed the threshold and are more than likely insulin-resistant or on the path. Since you cannot afford to take any chance of developing insulin resistance (IR) that leads to diabetes and subsequent stroke, the solution must be obvious—**kick your sugar habit starting today**. Once you appreciate how heart attack (HA) and stroke (S) rely on various conditioning agents that promote clot formation, you can immediately begin a prevention strategy discussed in Part 1 of this book.

6. Do not allow the functional side of your body to take over the responsibilities of the compromised side, as it certainly will try to do. Follow the advice of your physical therapist.

---

1   Clonus: Alternate involuntary muscular contraction and relaxation in rapid succession.

2   Foot drop: Paralysis or weakness of the dorsiflexor muscles of the foot and ankle, resulting in dragging of the foot and toes.

3   High Glycemic: High-glycemic foods are those that rate high on the glycemic index, a measure of the expected effects of different carbohydrate levels on blood glucose.

Try to discover patience as you wait for plasticity to repair your body. Nerve repair is measured in years, not in days.

7. Reversals in progress are going to occur – don't let it get you down.

8. If a new treatment modality shows up on the Internet or other advertising medium that convinces you it would be worth a try—before you buy into it, I suggest you contact the seller and ask one key question: Can you give me the name of a stroke center that is using your idea? Believe me; I have enough experience to know that if they can't name one, the product is suspect.

9. In terms of nutrients/supplements—there is no road map for their use. If you elect to use them, it boils down to what you think makes sense, but you will probably never be able to generate proof of a benefit. With that in mind, I use the following agents. If they are of interest, you should research them for details of purported benefits, risks, etc. Of course, get your doctor's approval before starting any supplement program; I make no specific endorsements.

- 1,000 mg/day magnesium citrate or other readily soluble form of magnesium
- 1,000 mg/day calcium, magnesium, potassium combo
- 588 mg/day acetyl carnitine capsule, plus 5 ml/day liquid carnitine
- Nattokinase 2,000 fibrinolytic unit capsule, vitamin K removed
- Antioxidants: lipoic acid 100 mg, vitamin C 2,000 mg, vitamin E 400 units, selenium 100 μg, taurine 1,000 mg, and CoQ10 100 mg
- One tablespoon flavored Nordic cod oil and 1,000 mg flax oil
- Lysine 500 mg.
- Vitamins: niacin, multi-, and vitamin D3.

- Iodine from Iodoral, Iosol, Lugol, or kelp is well worth your study and consideration.

Be very careful about consuming anything containing metals such as chromium, lead, manganese, mercury, or arsenic as they are all neurotoxic. It is important to recognize that there is a different set of rules for bodies that have a neurologic disease—they will respond with much greater sensitivity to neurotoxins according to my neuropathy theory and personal experience. Please seek your doctor's advice.

As an example, I notice that chromium picolinate is sometimes recommended for help in managing insulin resistance. I encourage caution for anyone with neurologic disease. You may want to talk with your doctor about this point of view but keep in mind this is not yet a proven issue. This is simply another case of deciding if what I say makes sense, and then taking charge of your own health decisions. Before leaving this scene, let me mention two non-metals also associated with neurotoxicity and both commonly used as a health supplements. These are iodine and selenium (both used in thyroid disease management). I have seen several internet supporting references to this point but leave it up to the reader to pursue if interested. Given the fact that one third of the world population live in an iodine deficient area with upwards of 95 percent deficient, yet given the powerful effect if iodine on breast cancer (Brownstein), this becomes a first class dilemma. The reader will need to make this call. Iodine toxicity comments relate only to subjects with history of neurologic disease.

If you have had a chance to review the section on nutrients/supplements, after reading about the many benefits of arginine, you may also want to learn more about it. I read the purported benefits of arginine in stimulating nitric oxide, as recorded in *NO More Heart Disease* by (Ignarro, 2005), and was sufficiently persuaded to try a product offered on the Internet called Cardio Cocktail, which was said to deliver five grams of arginine per dose. I tried it for a month at about eighty dollars per bottle, and could find no reason to continue the assessment.

Beyond that, I found that I am a member of a subset of about 20 percent of the population who experience activation of a latent herpes virus (fever blisters) associated with an imbalance between arginine and lysine. Were it not for this reaction, I think an arginine supplement could be useful.

PLEASE NOTE: AS WITH ALL INFORMATION OFFERED IN THIS BOOK, BEFORE USE, IT IS IMPERATIVE THAT YOU CHECK WITH YOUR DOCTOR, AS SEVERAL OF THESE SUPPLEMENTS CAN AFFECT BLOOD CLOTTING AND RESULT IN POTENTIAL DANGER—NATTOKINASE IS A POSSIBLE EXAMPLE.

10. Exercise

    Exercise is probably one of the most important yet least-practiced elements of post-stroke health maintenance. I think the trick is to find something that you enjoy doing while contributing to your body health. In my case, since I enjoy jogging, I do enough to maintain the ability to jog at least one mile nonstop. If you encounter someone who seems to walk faster than you can jog, not to worry; it is endurance, not speed, we are cultivating.

I also am insistent about regaining my pre-stroke push-up standard, which was 100 push-ups plus my age. Whereas immediately post-stroke I could not even do one push-up, on my 30-month post-stroke date, I did 150 pushups and will keep at it until I can do 180 or more by my three-year anniversary in August of 2010. Actually on June 20, 2010, I decided to take pressure off of myself by doing a hundred nonstop, followed by ten knee bends, followed by fifty push-ups, followed by ten more knee bends, then fifty more push-ups, for a total of two hundred. I say that is good enough for now. Heck, I'm past eighty—excuses, excuses! Next target: three hundred.

11. Another avenue I suggest is to get into a tai chi or yoga class, as these forms of exercise can be adapted for all physical

limitations and are universally recommended by therapists dealing with stroke. My tai chi teacher refers to our sessions in terms of "playing tai chi as a game". She made it a special experience, much anticipated each week.

As an exercise option, you may want to consider an exercise bicycle. You may find that you want to move your body but do not really feel like an outside activity. I found that while riding an exercise bicycle is not my favorite thing to do, it certainly will take the edge off the innate need to get moving. I found even five-minute intervals at maximum tension yields a satisfying experience, easily repeated as often as you wish, providing cumulative benefit. I purchased a Schwinn upright, model 120, and found the engineering outstanding at a cost of about $300. It offers a very smooth ride with on-board monitoring devices. I have not regretted the investment.

Hypothyroidism

Before leaving body response, here was one more surprise for me: post-stroke, I felt cold almost all of the time, keeping a mattress warmer on high when going to bed, and sitting with a heater beside my chair during the daytime. When I got into the study of myotonia—myotonic dystrophy, as reported in Part 1 of the book, I came across a paper called "Hypothyroidism Mimicking Myotonic Dystrophy" (Margolis, Freitas, Margolis 1973). This led me into a study of hypothyroid that also features cold intolerance, which finally brings me to the point I want to make: one result of hypothyroid and aging is that your body temperature may not register as 98.6 degrees, but lower. In my case, I had never checked temperature until 32 months post-stroke; at that point, I usually found it to be 97.4, and often at 96.8. What I am suggesting is that part of your health maintenance program should include a record of body temperature. A low reading (even a few tenths of degree) could give you a heads-up on hormonal changes, such as hypothyroidism that might be occurring post-stroke, as you age. I await blood studies to decide whether low thyroid is an issue. As written in Part 1 of the book however, I think my clinical evidence of hypothyroid is sufficiently persuasive that treatment should be offered on a trial basis.

From my reading of hypothyroid literature, it became evident that the usual biochemical changes associated with hypothyroid cannot be considered reliable indicators, as clinical observations become the index of choice. When you watch your muscle mass disappear and your skin age at an accelerated pace, along with cold intolerance, and persistent low body temperature, you have a pretty good clue that you may need some expert hormone advice.

Some of the Typical Symptoms for Hypothyroidism:

You need not have them all to qualify for hypothyroidism.

- Constipation
- Frequent desire to sleep, sense of fatigue
- Cold hands and feet
- Dry skin, accelerated wrinkling, brittle nails
- Elevated cholesterol and LDL[4]
- Arthritis-type pain
- Low body temperature (<98.6 F)
- Depression
- Difficulty losing weight—in my case difficulty maintaining weight
- Headaches
- Brain fog
- Fluid retention
- Stiff joints
- Muscle cramps
- Shortness of breath with exertion
- Possible chest pain
- Menstrual problems
- Sinusitis

---

4   LDL: Refers to low-density lipoprotein. It's also sometimes called "bad" cholesterol. Lipoproteins are made of fat and protein. They carry cholesterol, triglycerides, and other fats, called lipids, in the blood to various parts of the body.

- Iodine deficiency
- Frequent urination
- Hearing loss
- Raynaud's syndrome[5]
- Loss or thinning of outer one-third of eyebrow (Photographs of my mother confirm she had the pattern, and certainly had many of the hypothyroid symptoms listed as I recall.)

It is my understanding that using thyroid supplements without first excluding adrenal function as the issue is counterproductive. It can result in the thyroid putting extra stress on the adrenals, making them do more to accomplish less. This is a subject to discuss with an endocrinologist, if in doubt. Whatever the case, all the concern for thyroid and adrenal function is meaningless if the body has an iodine deficiency. Neither of the hormonal problems can be approached without adequate iodine, for which most people in the world are said to be deficient. Japanese people who consume adequate kelp are the exception. The message is that solving an iodine deficiency is the first order of business for symptoms of low thyroid/adrenal function. This subject is covered effectively in Brownstein's book on iodine.

From my perspective, there is little hope of overcoming fatigue and gradual loss of mobility without first overcoming depressed hormone production. This problem is at the top of my list of inconveniences at forty months post-stroke and is still a work in progress, but Lordy, what a grind in the meantime!

For those who deal with diabetes symptoms along with stroke, I want to point out that foot care is crucial, as is effective management of dry skin on the lower extremities. I found that daily application of sesame oil or mink oil does a good job keeping the skin from cracking—and it works on the scalp as well. Here is what can happen, according to Bernstein. The wound from attempted callus removal, for example,

---

5   Raynaud's syndrome: This is a condition in which the smallest arteries that bring blood to the fingers or toes constrict (go into spasm) when exposed to cold or from an emotional upset. The small veins are usually open, so the blood drains out of the capillaries. The result is that the fingers or toes become pale, cold, and numb.

can morph into loss of the foot, due to slow healing and infection—an all-too-common event among diabetics.

Taking an abrupt change in direction, in the next lessons are some of the mental aspects for post-stroke health management. While up to this point, my focus of attention has been on how the body responds to the post-stroke era, I next want to redirect our thoughts to how our mind trumps our bodily concerns. I have tried to present biochemical evidence that our thoughts create our reality. This is an empowering concept for anyone, whether recovering from disease or simply finding a way to live a more meaningful life.

The Practical Side Of Stroke

Introduction

My goal with this book is to reach as many people as possible, those who have had stroke events, and those who have not but are at risk of having one. (Did I leave anyone out?)

What I hope to do is point out what is generally known about stroke prevention and recovery, providing reference material, along with my own ideas to help each person decide for him- or herself the level of risk they are willing to accept and what they may want to consider minimizing their risk. A warning stroke is not a death sentence, but it sure is the most positive thing your body can do for you to alert you to your fate if neglected.

Post-Stroke Experience

Following my embolic shower type of stroke affecting my left side, the most surprising element of stroke management was my discovery that even if you experience some recovery within the first few months post-stroke, you must not assume you have a solid preview of the impact of stroke upon your life. Why? Well, it turned out that about eighteen months post-stroke, new symptoms appeared, which I came to believe were either progressive or delayed symptoms from the initial event. They manifested in several ways, such as modest swelling with redness of the affected foot and calf, as well as what seemed to be swollen muscles/tendons in the thigh. Also noted was a significant increase in reflexivity of the thigh muscles.

For example, I could sit with my knees drawn up and then tap a TV remote or similar implement on my thigh and cause the leg to straighten out as a reflex reaction. I also noted that the usually refreshing morning stretch had become unproductive with the sensation that those muscles could not stretch, since they seemed to be already tensed, as discussed in Part 1 of the book.

Here was another shocker that woke me up to reality. As I stood at the window to apply for a handicapped parking placard, the office manager asked if I needed a temporary or a permanent sign. Before I could answer, the nurse standing beside me said, "Oh, he needs a permanent sign." Wow! I was clearly thinking a temporary would do. That shock still persists—I just can't believe it.

Yet another manifestation of post-stroke events was the occurrence of clonus in the affected foot. Clonus was recognized as a modestly uncontrolled shaking of the foot during or following exercise of that limb, which returned to normal with rest. Also affected was my ability to walk for one to two miles without interruption. For the first year post-stroke, I had been able to make a relatively easy transition from the need for a walker, to a cane, to no assistance, and was able to walk and jog quite comfortably.

As I slowly and reluctantly acknowledged my delusion that recovery would be programmed on an upward trajectory, it was a significant blow to accept that we are not guaranteed an uninterrupted path to recovery, and indeed, things still could get worse. Even as I write this, at twenty-six months post-stroke, I face the possibility that I may never get any better. My point is not to offer a discouraging word on stroke recovery but rather to help cushion the surprises for others dealing with their recovery process and stroke management.

Stroke Recovery Self-Help

My first question was whether there is such a thing as self-help for stroke recovery. The main thrust of this portion of the book is to review the various treatment modalities recommended for stroke rehabilitation—both those approved and those not necessarily approved by vascular disease experts. I evaluated several modalities, which I have described, and tried to give a frank judgment of their utility and potential for contribution to stroke recovery. From my studies, there seems to be a consensus among stroke experts that stroke recovery can still occur years after the event, considering brain plasticity[1] never seems to give up on the body.

Given such a slow recovery process and no proven intervention avenue available, about all anyone can hang on to is hope that some new remedy will show up. In fact, with so much demand for help and so few resources, a new stroke victim will find a world of suggested remedies to tempt you—while absorbing your money. I intentionally bought into some of these alternatives so that I could document them for this book with my findings of those that seemed to be reasonable possibilities.

My goal was to give readers enough information to make their own judgment, while saving their time and money. The point of the major portion of this book is to share with readers the multiple avenues I have systematically pursued in trying to find something useful to affect stroke recovery or to alleviate some of the symptoms. Sometimes even mostly negative results are worth more than no data.

A Stroke Was My Teacher is offered for that category of the population who takes responsibility for their own health and chooses to look for solutions beyond those traditionally offered by the medical community. Readers attracted to this book are proactive and usually challenge medical dogma. We insist on finding out for ourselves the current state of medical knowledge. Of course, what we are really looking for is a doctor who will agree with his patient about the problem and the likely solution.

While the central focus is on stroke, the principles followed in my search for answers could easily apply to any health issue. I do point out the frustration of trying to get medical advice where anyone sufficiently informed to ask his or her doctor for evidence of proof for the advice is labeled either a smart aleck, a smart ass, or at the very least, a damned nuisance for those "inside-the-box" health professionals.

---

1   Brain plasticity: A term is used to refer the brain's unique ability to constantly change, grow, and remap itself over the course of a lifetime.

When you meet such a person who is not willing to listen to your point of view and immediately counters with a comment like, "I'm not going to debate you", you know you are dealing with an ego that is insecure. If male, he probably wears a shirt, tie, and coat in the examining room and seems to try to intimidate or ridicule, rather than accept an idea he had not considered.

Things My Mother Never Told Me

There are surprises to be encountered during the stroke experience. For example, proprioception was a new word to me, and it refers to your ability to sense the position, location, orientation, and movement of the body and its parts. If your stroke affects your proprioception—as it did with me—you will find that you may not sense where your hand is. For example, in my case I might be drinking a glass of water and realize I just spilled it in my lap, because I could not sense it was tilting unless I actually saw it happen.

Another example: salmon on a plank. While grilling salmon on my deck, it became necessary to upgrade the menu from grilled salmon to salmon on a plank, as the platter tipped on its way indoors, spilling the salmon onto the plank deck. I deftly returned the fish to the platter and took it inside for dinner, with no one the wiser. One must be very cautious with this type of problem, because it is no effort at all to put your hand on a hot surface without realizing. And incidentally, when touching an object, hot feels hotter and cold feels colder on the stroke-affected side of your body. And if you are using a blood thinner, such as Coumadin, you may feel chilly a good deal of the time.

Another stroke novelty is bladder urgency and bladder frequency, which may come as a total surprise. Having encountered that problem early in the recovery phase while using a walker, I decided to attach a plastic emergency jug to my walker while indoors, picturing the worst that could happen—and it was not long before it did. Believe me, when you've got to go with a stroke-challenged body, you have no time to select hydrant options.

As another cautionary note, impairment of leg function is sometimes recognized as shuffling or dragging of the affected foot. Without constant vigilance, you will soon find yourself tripping on floor mats and similar objects. The message is to take extra care when walking, because if you think things are bad now, just imagine how much worse they would be if you fall and are faced with a broken limb on top of your stroke issues.

Be extra careful walking at all times. Move slowly, pick up your affected foot when taking a step, climbing stairs, etc. It is easy to misstep, as you will find out.

On the other hand, some symptoms will improve with time, either with or without treatment, but you can vastly enhance your mental outlook if you can point to a sign of improvement as time goes by. Believe me, *any* sign of recovery is huge. At best, given the paucity of documented remedies to affect your recovery, about all you really have is whatever hope you can generate for yourself—and that is the difference between favorable mental health and depression.

Get that? Depression, for some, is a matter of choice—you decide what you want to think about, and with that choice will come freedom. Dwell on the negatives and you will live in the negative field, with all the nasty stuff that goes with it. Take golf, for instance. For the first year post-stroke, I could still get around for nine holes. Now, I can't hit the ball even up to my past low standards, but guess what: there is a sense of frustration totally gone from my life, and I rather enjoy that feature. Yes, of course my ego flinches when I use a driver on a par three.

Let me hasten to add that for some, depression may not be a choice. In the work of D. J. Amen in his book called *Change Your Brain, Change Your Life,* he reveals how metabolic or even structural abnormalities can show up on SPECT (Single Photon Emission Computed Tomography) brain scans that allow experts to pinpoint location of defects and then offer targeted remedy. He has successfully dealt with anxiety, depression, obsessiveness, anger, and impulsiveness, among other problems.

The General Pattern of Embolic Stroke

The general picture that emerges after a stroke is to hang on to your hat, because each stroke predicts the next. While this may not always be true, it is enough of a warning that any prudent victim will want to know what can be done to prevent another stroke, and whether there is anything that can be done to accelerate recovery after the stroke.

Before these avenues can be explored, one would like to know, if possible, the cause of the initial embolic stroke. Causes seem to fall broadly into two categories. Cause one is said to be the result of a blood clot that formed in the heart, associated with *atrial fibrillation.* You will notice that I have challenged that notion in the first part of the book, dealing with the mechanism of S and HA. The pathway for cause two for embolic stroke is the release of plaque and its clot that formed in an artery serving the brain.

To prevent subsequent stroke you should know your prevention target. If it is thought to have originated in the heart, then you will need a blood thinner (Coumadin), and a full complement of anti-inflammatory agents, with magnesium as the most important as described in Part One of the book dealing with the schematic and its interpretation.

The second prevention strategy, if it is believed to be plaque-related, is that in addition to blood thinner and anti-inflammatory agents, you may want to consider a full complement of antioxidants. At this stage of my understanding, these are the only things currently promoted to minimize the arterial inflammation that causes plaque and thus the blockage that leads to stroke or heart attack if it goes that direction. If your stroke was determined to originate in the heart—which is not easily established—you will find that a magnesium citrate supplement along with flax oil can have a dramatic effect on arrhythmia, if your body reacts as mine did.

The third main pattern of stroke is hemorrhagic, where a blood vessel ruptures in the brain, preventing oxygen from reaching all portions of the brain. It should be clear to you by now that all types of stroke have one thing in common: they prevent oxygen and nutrients from reaching all parts of the brain.

Critical Realities for Both Prevention and Recovery

Rule Number One: *A stroke is an oxygen emergency, and a stroke is a dehydration emergency.* Don't ever forget this, and don't ever let your health care provider overlook this.

So once you think you have a good idea of what caused your stroke, you may be ready to plan a course of action toward prevention and recovery.

Different Strokes for Different Folks

What makes stroke management so complicated is that no two people have the same symptoms or deficits. This becomes clear when you consider the following facts (*Scientific American Book of the Brain* 1999:3).

It is commonly accepted that eighty percent of all strokes are classified as ischemic, which means they are the result of a migrated blood clot that may have originated in a blood vessel supplying the brain or from a clot that formed in the heart associated with an irregular heartbeat (referred to as an arrhythmia or as atrial fibrillation or A Fib). You will note from the schematic interpretation in Part 1 of the book that I have questioned A Fib as causing strokes.

Apparently, according to some thinking, even the seemingly innocent ventricular missed-beat pattern is enough to invite the potential for clot formation. Those who give serious attention to skipped beats are in a minority, as I read the literature. The blood supplies to the brain serve approximately a trillion nerve-related cells (100 billion of them neurons).

The death of any focal group of neurons is caused by blocked access of the neurons to oxygen and nutrients, as previously mentioned. Blood reaches the brain through either of the carotid arteries, which immediately makes it a 50:50 chance as to which side of the brain will receive the clot, and thus which opposite side of the body will manifest the damage. From discussion on chemotaxis in Chapter 4 in Part 1, you will note that I no longer believe chance is involved.

The significance of pathway choices is that it points up the random nature of stroke events, since a clot can stop at any convenient branch of a blood vessel to affect a stroke. Thus, indeed, different folks have different strokes, and it is impossible to predict the outcome or treatment protocol for any victim. Every person is unique, requiring stroke-management strategies unique to each individual.

This scenario does tell us one thing, however, and that is, if you can prevent unwanted clot formation, you have at least an 80 percent chance to minimize an ischemic stroke event. As the central message of this book, we discussed possible strategies to minimize unwanted clot formation, within the lessons dealing with nutrients and/or supplements, dehydration, arrhythmia, and insulin resistance.

What you cannot predict is where the clot is going to land and what will be the casualty. A positive intervention for stroke has been achieved with the use of the clot-busting drug tPA[2] when used in time, but it also carries notable risk for causing bleeding in the brain. The upshot of this story is that any strategy for treatment must be precisely tailored for each stroke patient. The paths used for physical therapy, for example, may bear no resemblance from one person to another, since each may manifest unique damage patterns.

One problem I have noted is that many doctors seem to think that if you have seen a neurologist, you have seen a stroke specialist. If that is true, we are in deep trouble.

As an example, I asked one neurologist if my issue of bladder frequency and bladder urgency could be stroke-related. Stunningly, while I had a literature search page in my pocket showing 133,000 relevant articles linking bladder issues with stroke—this neurologist insisted there was no connection with stroke, and that, "You must have something else going on." So much for experts.

---

2   tPA: Tissue plasminogen activator (tPA) is a thrombolytic agent (clot-busting drug). It's approved for use in certain patients having a heart attack or stroke.

You May Never Get a Second Chance to Prevent a Stroke

Take this advice to the bank: if you ignore the warning given to you by TIA event(s), you are on the path to a life-changing experience for you and all those around you.

From my perspective, I think that when you ignore the TIA warning, it is just like holding a gun to your head and then asking yourself if the bullet would actually kill you. While every instinct may tell you that almost everyone who has pulled the trigger in that circumstance did indeed meet their demise; that is reason enough for most people. However, you must realize that the person who has had one or more TIAs and ignores them, either with or without medical supervision, has in effect already pulled the trigger and will meet their demise (full-blown stroke) with virtually the same certainty as the gun holder. There simply is no second chance in either scenario. They are equally lethal, both in theory and in practice.

In terms of my experience, I had no idea a TIA could be so instructive, until a subsequent unequivocal stroke put it all into focus—a tad late for this dimwit. Actually, if our first encounter is not lethal, our bodies have given us a huge gift in the form of a warning stroke.

When you think about it, we all very likely may have experienced silent warning strokes, since recovery can occur within minutes or hours of an event. Given that we sleep about one-third of our lives, it is probably more surprising *not* to find brain lesions indicative of stroke than to find lesions. My three warning messages were entirely obscured by ego and a stubborn mindset that put them in the category of irrelevant. How stupid can one person be?

But here is a gift for you. Having now become aware of the gravity of a warning stroke—for heaven's sake don't manage your health status with dumb luck. Assume the worst-case outcome and demand—yes, I said *demand*—physician corrective action, for anything even resembling a warning stroke.

Throughout the book, I have discussed topics, sometimes humorous ones that reflect my practical experiences and what I think stroke candidates can anticipate if they are faced with the problem. I have tried to shape this into a "how to prevent stroke and heart attack" reference as well—going beyond current thinking.

According to my theory of neuropathy mechanism presented in this text, if you experienced a neurologic insult prior to or even after your stroke, you will just have to tough it out and accept that whatever initial damage was done to the nervous system is likely to re-manifest following an embolic stroke. According to my theory, a history of infections with any of the herpes group of viruses including chicken pox and Epstein-Barr, as well as non-herpes agents such as poliovirus or any other type of agent that is attracted to nerve tissue (such as an antibiotic like Cipro, a statin drug, or a food such as sugar or even excess oxygen), could be significant factors in how and if neuropathy manifests.

Difference Between Being Alive and Living After a Stroke

The effects of stroke are perverse and reckless in how they affect the medical victim as well as the care victim(s). Thus, we must constantly remind ourselves that while a relatively small portion of our bodies may seem to have died, the remainder of our being is still very much alive.

Whatever capabilities were not lost to stroke effect should be identified and appreciated, in terms of presenting ourselves as useful and productive beings. Don't be fooled, though; after a debilitating stroke, it would be very easy simply to throw in the towel by accepting your disability. It would be easy to look at life inward, rather than looking outward to focus on being alive and how to use your energy to resume and create new ways for actually living.

So here is the trick: let your mind and body know who is boss by first taking measure of the needs of others who require attention. This can be through churches, social services, hospitals, etc., wherever volunteers are needed. Become absorbed in others who have a tougher road than you, and let your limitations serve as example and inspiration for others. Demand that your body ignore self-concern and its ego. Assure yourself that anyone can sit around and grouse about fate, but there are damned few who are willing to overcome that path and accept a new mission cheerfully.

Here is a personal account of what I'm proposing. After completing my research career at Pfizer, although I had many satisfying accomplishments when looking back, I commented to anyone who cared to listen that I never felt I had done my life's work; this bugged me for years, thinking something big was still missing. Then came a stroke, and I realized I had the tools to try to fill in some of the gaps in understanding and managing stroke. This was an exciting revelation, because I now had a mission to pursue what could possibly be my life's work—at last. It just took a stroke to put me on the path. Ever hear of anyone who could readily accept that they had a stroke? Well, here is one.

As an example of living after stroke, for my eightieth birthday, my wife Sylvia arranged a European river cruise on the Rhine, Mein, and Danube Rivers. Naturally I was a little concerned whether I would be able to negotiate the demands of such a fifteen-day trip. In short, it was a magnificent experience in living, with breathtaking scenery, postcard little towns, castles, and vineyards. What a sight—on one day, I decided to stay on board ship rather than do a walking tour. When some of the men returned, I chided them by relating how while they were away, I saw a beach where every woman was topless. It was sort of a private joke when I told them that they failed to ask the key question: "How many were there?" Answer: one. If you decide to do such an excursion, probably a seven-to-ten-day version would be just fine; if you can arrange to travel with friends, all the better.

You will soon realize what you have been missing when you sense the difference between being alive and living, post-stroke. We traveled with my niece Judie and her retired army colonel husband, George Giles. Their youth and enthusiasm were the catalysts for a treasured experience. And guess what, the long travel requirements fade to irrelevant as your memories replace the grinding health and caretaking concerns.

Believe me, your next doctor's appointment will be the last thing on your mind while you are living your life.

Taking Anxiety Out of Stroke Recovery

There is anxiety with the seemingly ever-changing landscape of stroke symptoms, where new ones (such as burning, itching, and sensitivity to touch) seem to appear, and the intensity of original symptoms seems to be in flux. Also, you will find the sensation of a numb or swollen foot or ankle, for example, ranging from a predictable and constant feeling to one with wide variation in degree of those sensations, depending on the day, time of day, diet, age, or some undefined factors. I have developed a new strategy for dealing with stroke, based upon "what if I'm right" and "what if I'm wrong" theses—a strategy that emerged at my two-year stroke anniversary.

I came to believe that rather than noticing the appearance of possible new symptoms, and vagaries in existing symptoms, I shall take the position that ultimately the forces of plasticity will prevail, resolving my deficits, and that I will accept that notion with full confidence of outcome. Jill Bolte Taylor in her book, *My Stroke of Insight,* needed eight years to recover function and resume teaching after her hemorrhagic stroke. I know of a patient who needed about five years for her hand to unfold following a stroke—both consistent with the capacity of the brain to form new nerve pathways (plasticity). At this point, two years post-stroke, each new sensation that occurs is simply added to, and then left in, my mental catalogue of probable plasticity events to be resolved.

IF I AM RIGHT, then all of the daily anxiety will be removed while I simply accept what is, live in the moment, and become less concerned about what I can do to accelerate or ameliorate the recovery process—which to this point has been zero anyway.

IF I AM WRONG, and my condition regresses or deteriorates, with no eventual improvement, then I shall have lost nothing beyond daily anxiety along the way and will have enjoyed my late years with peace of mind and a positive attitude and hopefully become (even) easier to live with. (Ahem) I reserve the right and intention to continue a vigorous pursuit of stroke study, no matter what.

Stroke and the Aging Body

One of the frustrating aspects of dealing with the effects of stroke is to distinguish stroke effects from the effects of normal aging of the body. While this may seem like a minor issue, as most stroke subjects are among the mature population, I assure you that distinguishing the contribution of aging from stroke effects is not minor. It is very real and deserves undivided attention. As I experience the combination of events, I find a tendency to attribute to stroke, symptoms that are documented signs of the aging process. Please note—you will find little comfort from a visit to a doctor who has been asked essentially to suggest a remedy for old age. Actually, I have become an unintended authority on this package, since I am now past eighty and into my third year of study on post-stroke effects.

If the reader is inclined to sort out the distinctions of stroke and aging, I suggest you first start by reading an excellent account of the *Biology of Human Aging* by Alexander P. Spence (1999), wherein he organizes the process into how aging affects us at the cellular level and goes on to describe effects of age on each of the body systems, starting with the skin and working deeper through muscular, skeletal, nervous, circulatory, immune, respiratory, digestive, urinary, reproductive, and endocrine systems. This fine book will give you a comprehensive overview of how and why aging affects each of these systems. To find a compendium of all possible stroke effects is more challenging, and in my opinion, an impossible task.

When you realize that a stroke can hit and possibly destroy any of a hundred billion or more neurons, with each neuron apparently assigned to a particular body function, then it becomes obvious that no two strokes are necessarily alike and indeed will probably be very unlike. Since it is not possible to predict which neurons will be hit out of all the possibilities, the symptoms present after a stroke in one person may resemble symptoms in another stroke victim only in the most general terms.

The one area of concern that needs to be emphasized after experiencing a stroke, combined with an aging body, is the real possibility that your stroke symptoms may be related to hormonal changes resulting in hypothyroid, for example. Since this was indeed my experience, it needs to be on your list of potential events to which you and your doctor should remain alert. (Discussed in Lesson Four.)

A Stroke Experience Recap

Stop the clot is the goal! According to my hypothesis, red cells clump when they become preconditioned by any of several factors. I have identified several microbial agents in detail that have that potential, as does out-of-balance fibrinogen, or a magnesium deficiency. So what contributes to these upsets? A case is made showing how dehydration is at the root of the problem. As we age, we lose our sense of thirst and become dehydrated with no warning signs.

Even if you have a family history of these vascular diseases, you can change your path by lowering blood pressure, staying well hydrated, including food choices that favor those rich in anti-oxidants, getting plenty of daily exercise, and—as a crucial element, a point is made why you *must* get sugar-sweet foods out of your life—forever, to avoid insulin resistance[3].

In the same line of thinking, while old age is said to be a non-modifiable risk factor for stroke, I say WHOA! If the aging subject had been adequately informed of the penalty for not drinking enough water, then as the aging process matured, in my opinion, the subject would have been much less likely to have experienced the stroke, heart attack, Alzheimer's disease, or many other illnesses. It is obvious that not all of the elderly become victims of stroke or heart attack—if old age, per se, is really a non-modifiable risk factor, how come so many older folks never experience those events?

Red cells and platelets eventually start sticking together if you become magnesium deficient, but here is the hidden surprise—*if you become insulin resistant* (IR), *your magnesium supply becomes depleted* (Linus Pauling Institute of Oregon State University Information Sheet; Durlach, J., Magnesium and Aging).

---

3 Insulin resistance: (IR) is a physiological condition where the natural hormone insulin becomes less effective at lowering blood sugars. The resulting increase in blood glucose may raise levels outside the normal range and cause adverse health effects.

Stroke ER: What Was And What Should Have Been

The treatment programs I experienced after TIA's and a stroke in the emergency rooms, both in Florida and in North Carolina, were remarkably similar in strategy and execution. On each ER occasion, the strategy was … there was no strategy—no treatment whatsoever of any description. In Florida, they did at least hang an oxygen loop around my neck, whereas in North Carolina, incredibly, there was no oxygen administered—was I supposed to ask for it? Or perchance did they not follow protocol, or perchance was there no protocol to follow for such occasions? Someone important, who perhaps is rich or famous with a life considered worth saving, should ask some tough questions, in case they are faced with a stroke ER experience one day. Could adequate oxygen be the difference between manifesting a TIA (warning stroke) and having a for-real stroke?

Whatever the bitter facts, I feel free to offer my opinion of what should happen as a minimum ER effort.

1. As soon as appropriate test results exclude a hemorrhagic stroke event (MRA-magnetic resonance angiography), (CAT scan-computerized axial tomography), etc., ***the stroke patient should receive maximum oxygen and not be fooled by what a finger blood oxygen shows—it's the brain that needs the oxygen, not the finger.*** If there is no reliable way to gauge brain oxygen, then go for the ultimate. Put the patient in a hyperbaric oxygen chamber where there

is some level of certainty that the patient will not be oxygen-deprived at this critical time. Remember—*a stroke is an oxygen emergency*—if you remember nothing else.

2. The patient should receive an IV infusion of an appropriate magnesium salt, as discussed below.

3. Before and after reaching the ER, start forcing all the water you can handle (two to three glasses), and continue for the next three days and nights. Then make that part of your daily living routine—at least an extra two quarts per day. Remember—*a stroke is a water emergency.*

4. I think in addition to magnesium that taurine, acetyl carnitine, arginine, alpha lipoic acid, inositol, and aspirin should be given consideration as soon as practical and continued indefinitely.

5. If there are agents known to reduce cerebral edema and to stimulate cerebral blood flow, they should be considered.

6. Naturally, there are medications needed post-stroke to discourage clot formation, such as the blood thinner Coumadin, and in my opinion, alongside of Coumadin, consideration given for use of Nattokinase, a fibrinolytic enzyme.

Brain Swelling

There is a facet of stroke recovery that came as a total surprise to me. It turns out that after brain injury of any type, including stroke, the brain responds by swelling. The swelling itself can contribute to the impairment you experience post-stroke. It seems to me that this can yield the effect of a moving target for recovery. The more swelling and the longer in effect, the more chance for the appearance of new symptoms.

Here is one astonishing reality: at no time during my recovery process did a single doctor ever suggest that I should be examined for evidence of swelling, nor was there ever any type of interdiction even considered, to my knowledge, for that possibility. Had I known that swelling is an expected stroke-related event, I would have insisted on an answer to that question. When you don't even know enough about stroke to realize that swelling is a potential issue and then insist on treatment if indicated, it becomes an intractable problem for those of us who try to be a partner in our health management. This is an outrageous facet of health care that elicits an expletive every time it comes back to mind.

With the strong anti-inflammatory, anti-red-cell-stickiness, and anti-arrhythmia properties of magnesium salts, there would seem to be little risk with the administration of a good oral dose of something like magnesium citrate as a first intervention step in the ER. The main side effect would be diarrhea, a small price to pay. As I think about this subject from a different direction, it seems to me that subjects with rheumatoid arthritis would find benefit from daily use of a magnesium salt, using the same reasoning as for stroke.

Here is one idea for ERs that seems so obvious, it cannot be for real. I am thinking about head/brain trauma from sports, from stroke and any other circumstance where inflammation resulting in brain swelling could occur.

Emergency Room Suggestion

Before I discuss the idea, I need to ask whether we have a reliable way to detect brain swelling. Since a family member returned from her physical exam with the pronouncement from her doctor that he could not see any evidence of brain swelling, I judge there is some way to make that assessment. The idea is this: In the management of strains, sprains, and all other inflammatory processes, the first thought is to apply ice. Following that thought process, why would we not have a helmet with cooling coils available for brain trauma patients, which could be immediately worn in the ER to minimize brain swelling? If not already evaluated, this idea would seem to merit the attention of NINDS by following a cohort with and without brain cooling. Am I just too dumb to see the fallacy in this idea?

The Intuitive Side Of Stroke Recovery

Our bodies seem to have infinite wisdom, which in my experience manifests as a persistent urge to do something physical to help the recovery process. In my case, the first night in the hospital following my stroke, I felt compelled to get out of bed and do deep knee bends and push-ups, which I did in the middle of the night. I later found out that the physical therapist would indeed recommend that sort of activity, believing that such motion can be helpful for physical deficits like mine. It is of course, impossible to know if my compulsion actually served any purpose—but I can say it did no harm while giving me the sense I was doing something to help myself.

As a more dramatic example, while on a European river cruise in August of 2009 (two-year stroke anniversary) I met a gentleman from New Zealand who volunteered that he had experienced several heart attacks and strokes. His name is John Fowles (pictured at end of this lesson).

He gave me permission to share his experience in this book. John had three heart attacks by age fifty-nine, and now at age sixty-two, he has had three strokes. His symptoms included angina and atrial fibrillation. He has three heart zone stents, and his stroke occurred at a time when his wife had recently died of cancer and he was at a high work-related stress level. His first stroke left him with double vision, with one eye looking to the left and down while the other eye looked to the right and upward. John intuitively reasoned that he needed to create a condition that would force the eyes to focus on a single object simultaneously. To achieve that goal, he secured a small low-level trampoline and placed a large letter E on his garage wall. He gently bounced on the trampoline for ten minutes each day for a year, starting out by covering his stronger eye and then fixing his eye on the letter E while bouncing. He began to see benefits within three months.

Remarkably, without any other intervention or help, he was able to train his eyes to achieve vision alignment, which still persists. As another example of his intuitive capacity, he reasoned that his loss of artistic appreciation might be helped by singing in a barbershop quartet, which was also successful. Finally, to improve memory, he got a book of jokes and measured his memory improvement by reading and recalling jokes, judging his success by whether the punch line elicited a response. While John may be in a select group who have special intuitive capacity, his story should give comfort and hope to the large company of stroke victims who seem to have no hope beyond whatever they can manage to generate for themselves.

The Philosophical Side Of Stroke

Truth in a Tuning Fork

If one subscribes to the aphorism that our thoughts create our reality, it is but a small step to appreciate how each of us, as a center of energy, reacts with one another by energy transfer. The perfect example in the physical world is one in which, when a tuning fork is struck to emit its wave frequency (energy signature), it causes every other fork of the same frequency design to resonate with the first fork. The second fork emits the same frequency as the initiating fork by virtue of absorption and transfer of energy—***without ever physically touching the second fork.***

This simple reality yields a full explanation of the type of interactions exchanged by sentient beings.

Example One: As we experience the stimuli provided by our senses, we involuntarily and immediately react to all forms of stimuli contained in the spiritual, in people, places, and things. Each stimulus has its own energy signature that we can associate with such things as music, art, and people, in either a positive, neutral, or negative manner. Those beings who emit an energy pattern (frequency or signature) complementary to the outside stimulus will perceive that stimulus as a positive experience, while those who emit a conflicting frequency will perceive the stimulus in a negative context. The degree of resonance or dissonance will determine the intensity of our feelings about the stimuli. The ultimate level of resonance will appear as profound love for the stimulus.

Example Two: Have you ever walked into a room and sensed a negative atmosphere? Or perhaps noticed when someone else entered the room, the person brought negativity in with them? Or maybe you inexplicably and immediately feel a very strong bond with someone, even at first meeting. This phenomenon was nicely documented in the book by Dr. Jill Bolte Taylor called *My Stroke of Insight*. Jill, as a neuroscientist, detailed her experience while recovering from a devastating hemorrhagic stroke that revealed to her the positive and the negative energy patterns of those around her.

Since in my view, our thoughts do in fact create our reality—we must be very careful of what and whom we think about, since once strongly affected by stimuli, either in a positive or negative way, it can have a profound effect on how we conduct our lives and how we affect those around us. We have a sacred responsibility for the life of others, as well as for ourselves. Our reaction to energy stimuli is neither good nor bad. They are also neither right nor wrong, simply put; they are what they are, and should be recognized as such.

Other Examples: How about the way animals respond to us, based on whether we project fear or confidence? Is this not also a perfect example of resonance with our energy signature? There have been numerous times when, for example, I willed a bird or a butterfly to land on my hand or a chipmunk in the woods to sit on my lap. These events are real and point to the common energy forces among all sentient beings. I recall once when I heard the collie next door start to howl like a wolf, and I wondered if the dog was signaling an earthquake or some natural event. And yes indeed, that is precisely what was going on, I later learned—although an event was never felt.

When I went fishing frequently years ago, I got the impression that when fishing from a boat, if I had fish on a stringer, I was less likely to catch fish as easily as when there were no fish on the stringer. I judged that fish can communicate distress and alarm. When I finally got to the point that I hoped I would not catch a fish, I stopped the "sport". To illustrate how energy transfer from plants to humans occurs, I draw your attention to a fascinating book called *The Secret Life of Plants* by Peter Tompkins and Christopher Bird (1973). They provide numerous examples where plants sense human intention and respond to human thought. Here is an example of plant-human interaction: An IBM lab worker picked three tree leaves and daily transmitted mental thoughts of survival to two leaves ignoring the third. After a week he observed the ignored leaf as brown and shriveled, while the leaves receiving affectionate thoughts remained green. I successfully confirmed the experiment. This book puts our lives into perspective in a hurry and is a recommended read.

The point of this discourse is a reminder that you do not need a life-changing health event to grasp the opportunity for each of us to relate to others as family with energy signatures identical with ours. It seems to me that recognizing our fundamental nature in terms of interacting energy fields is the essence of the true future of health care strategy. I first noticed this phenomenon through a therapist employing esoteric energy manipulation. This concept is so foreign to most health care workers that it will likely require many years to approach mainstream.

Let me give you an example of what I am talking about. Those who are skilled in energy therapy (esoteric energy) such as Coral Thorsen of the Spirit of the Mountains Retreat and the Center for Integrative Healing—both in the Brevard area, North Carolina, are able to sense the etheric patterns of energy surrounding each of us. With that skill, she can sense energy imbalances and restore them. She has not only healed herself from lupus, MS, cancer and other issues, but she has been able to direct conventional physicians to the source of patient problems otherwise characterized as idiopathic. Coral insists that hers is not a special gift, and in fact she offers teaching seminars for those who wish to learn. I can testify that it is a life-changing experience to one day be comfortably focused in a three-dimensional existence and then be thrust into an entirely new and foreign but welcome sense of being. Ignore at your peril, in my judgment.

To accept the concept of energy as the center of our being, it would be useful for the reader to become familiar with the work of McTaggart called *The Field-The Quest for the Secret Force of the Universe* and the work of Gary Zukav in his book titled *The Dancing Wu Li Masters*. This work provides an excellent understandable overview of quantum physics. In fact, the title translated from Chinese defines Wu Li as "patterns of organic energy."

To further grasp how everyone and everything is part of the same energy field, we can benefit by considering the concept of the universe as a hologram, as described by Talbot (1991) in the book *The Holographic Universe*. A hologram, as described by Talbot on pages 15 and 16 "is produced when a single laser light is split into two separate beams. The first is bounced off the object to be photographed (an apple).Then the second beam is allowed to collide with the reflected light of the first, and the resulting interference pattern is recorded on film. A piece of the holographic film is composed of irregular ripples, known as interference patterns. However, when the film is illuminated with another laser, a three-dimensional image of the original object (apple) appears. The unique aspect is that every small fragment of the piece of holographic film contains all the information recorded in the whole."

It was noted that depending on the angle of the laser beam, a single film can encode extremely dense records of information. Thus, since our memories are non-local, according to Pibram (1971, 1993), it appears that we search our memories for retrievable information by willfully changing our energy pattern so that the encoded records can surface successfully.

It seems to work something like this: as we might be trying to recall a name, it is sometimes helpful to go through the alphabet, which provides numerous angles for our thought energy to seek the matching resonance or holographic angle we need for perfect recall. This is my simplistic interpretation, anyway, and since no one knows for sure how this works, my idea is as good as the next, it seems to me.

The point here is that we can subconsciously both provide and recover mental images, creating our own reality by incorporating the principles of interference and resonance framed in a holographic context. Our challenge is to refine our capacity to emit multiple energy signatures as needed to access complementary energy signals throughout the universe.

As a personal example, while engaged in research for thirty-seven years, I often felt that my research ideas were not really mine; it was more as if I were a conduit or receiver for cosmic sources of information. I recall on several occasions, I received what I thought was a great idea, started a research project, only to discover several months later that the "new idea" turned up in a publication. Another circumstance comes to mind along that line, which is how remarkably close in time that the major literature search tools PubMed and Google came to public notice (within a year of each other).

My most recent example of tuning in to the universe occurred about one to two years ago when I received the idea that the shelf life of produce could be extended if I could find a way to capture ethylene as it is produced by the fruits and vegetables. I tried numerous strategies but was unable to come up with a practical solution. About six months later, a product came out on the market in which bags were made with a carbon absorbent impregnated and has been successfully marketed, extending the shelf life of produce.

What this discourse is intended to convey is that from a philosophical point of view, the only constant in our lives is change itself. Following stroke or any other type of trauma, our new assignment is to learn from the experience, endorse it, and find a positive message within it to help guide others if possible.

The Spiritual Side of Stroke

This lesson unfolds from a beginning where, on more than one occasion, my therapist/teacher for esoteric healing, Coral Thorsen, said to me, "Jim, you cannot believe how many spirits of doctors and scientists surround you, helping with your research." A perfect example of the presence of spirit in this process is where I was directed to the work of Albert Sabin, the father of live polio vaccine. I was reviewing literature for support of my neuropathy hypothesis described in Chapter 4, when I came across the report by Sabin in 1947 called *The Puzzler in Polio Epidemics*. He states, "No circumstance in the history of poliomyelitis is so baffling as its change during the past 50 years from a sporadic to an epidemic disease." Dr. Sabin, who lived in nearby Cincinnati, Ohio, at the time, visited our laboratories in Terre Haute, Indiana, on several occasions; indeed, I had met him to discuss polio, although not on an "Albert and Jim" basis.

We were making Salk polio vaccine at the time and doing some preliminary work on live vaccine simultaneously. My assignment in those days was responsibility for the safety and efficacy of the inactivated vaccine. Our paths crossed again indirectly in the late 1950s, since at that time I worked with our UK laboratories, where we became the first company to be licensed to make live vaccine on a commercial scale. I guess you could say he may have been tracking me for several years.

The point I am developing is that I was directed to his 1947 paper as discussed in Chapter 4 on neuropathy hypothesis. In that report, Sabin made the astute observation that polio epidemics have occurred with the greatest frequency and severity in the high sugar-consuming countries. I made note in that chapter that Sabin came within an eyelash of hitting my hypothesis squarely.

Here is the spiritual side of this saga, as I interpret it. Sabin died in 1993 and had unfinished business that he carried into the spiritual world, never having solved the baffling polio problem. He found in my studies a vehicle that offered an explanation for his troubling issue, a vehicle that would allow his work to resurface and be recognized for his remarkable insight on the role of sugar in this neurologic disease. It seems to me that spiritual help is clearly a now-obvious integral part of the lives of all sentient beings—in case we did not know it.

How Thoughts Create Our Reality

An important thrust of this book is the attention given to the general thesis that our thoughts create our realities. This proposition was bought into focus in the outstanding book by Bruce Lipton (2008) called *The Biology of Belief.* Central to his description is how our biology is connected with our beliefs. He asserts that our genes historically have been credited with control of the characteristics that define us as human beings, including our health and life span. He introduces us to another layer of genetic control through the agency of epigenes.

Lipton noted that only 5 percent (or less) of human health issues can be attributed to defective genes; 95 percent (or more) of issues are impacted by the functional control exercised by our epigenes. What this amounts to is a new paradigm where the decision of which of our structural genes are expressed depends upon the timing of signals issued from our epigenes to our structural genes. After the structural genes receive instructions, they then start producing the biochemical they were designed to make.

But here is the crucial question framed and answered by Lipton: what is the mechanism by which epigenes are activated? And the answer is that our epigenes are put in motion *by our thoughts*. So there you have it, as I interpret Lipton—since our epigenes activate our genes and our epigenes are activated by our thoughts—our thoughts thus create our reality. Think thoughts of fear, for example, and you activate genes that produce the hormones cortisol and adrenalin. If, on the other hand, you think thoughts or feel emotions of love, your genes start producing the hormone oxytocin, which has the exact opposite effect on our bodies.

So how do we produce more oxytocin? Numerous activities produce more oxytocin, such as meditation, yoga, exercise, massage, caring for a pet, joining a support group, or worshipping. One of the most important activities as described in *Love & Survival* by Dean Ornish is love and intimacy. So why not take a pill?

The main reason is that oxytocin cannot cross the blood-brain barrier[1]. Interestingly, the more oxytocin we make, the stronger our body and mind respond to it. Love tends to breed more love, as fear breeds more fear. A comprehensive look at neurochemicals can be found in the book *Molecules of Emotion* by Candice Pert (1997).

Thoughts and Reality in Quantum Physics

To grasp the notion that our thoughts create our reality, it is useful to peek into the world of quantum physics. What you will notice is that all you will find is nothingness. Quantum physicists observe that if you reduce an electron structure to the limit of test sensitivity, you will find the electron has no measurable dimension.

---

1   Blood brain barrier: The blood-brain barrier (BBB) is a cellular and metabolic barrier located at the capillaries in the brain that alters permeability, restricting the passage of some chemicals.

Adding to the mystery, depending on how you observe it, the electron can appear as a particle or as a wave. If you are convinced you are looking at a particle, then it will look like a particle. However, if you are convinced you are looking at a wave, then it will appear as a wave. (See last page of Final Lesson.)

So there you have it—according to experts in quantum physics, our thoughts create our reality, as I interpret their findings.

Taking this to practical example, we can refer to Talbot's illustration in his book, *The Holographic Universe.* Therein is described the work of Simonton, an oncologist, who led a terminal cancer patient to recovery by teaching the patient relaxation and mental imaging techniques. Basically the patient pictured the irradiation he was receiving as bullets of energy that immobilized the cancer cells, allowing white cells to carry the dead cells to points of removal in the liver and kidney.

This study led to the work of Achterberg (1988) as reported in *Imagery in Healing,* detailing numerous successes associated with imagery. It is not uncommon to find current examples in the literature of the use of imagery for illnesses. Our minds have the capacity to create our reality in matters of health and healing.

Byrne (2006) expanded this feature of our innate powers in the popular book under the title of *The Secret.*

The Purpose of Disease

Here is a simple message that explains a lot. The message is: the purpose of your disease is to put you on a spiritual path.

Your disease is an echo from the universe. The universe is perfection, and as a part of the universe, you are guided to achieve perfection one step at a time. The more serious your disease, the stronger is the message. Embrace your station in life and learn.

There are many books on this subject, but just consider the one by Louise Hay (2010) titled *You Can Heal Your Life.* This book is an international bestseller of 30 million copies; think of it—her message is so powerful that 30 million readers were directed to her to buy her book (mine included). You can also look at work of Alan Hopking (2009), titled *Esoteric Healing,* page 2, where he states, "by taking on disease, a person opens up to greater soul awareness."

Just talk to anyone who has faced a serious illness and you will find a soul who found their way to a spiritual path. A perfect example again is Coral Thorsen, who practices and teaches esoteric healing in Brevard, North Carolina, as previously mentioned.

Delayed-Progressive Stroke Symptoms

An Internet search for delayed-progressive stroke symptoms will yield reports that usually refer to the lacunar[1] subtype of strokes. One can come across this category of stroke when investigating the reason why new stroke symptoms appeared to manifest at eighteen months post-stroke, which I seemed to have experienced. I keep this discussion qualified by "seem to" and "appear to," for as you read on, you will discover that while this category of stroke *does* exist, there may be other reasons why one may sense regression of progress during stroke recovery.

In my case, at eighteen months post-stroke, I noticed more numbness in both the hand and foot, as well as swelling/redness of the foot on the stroke-affected side of my body, with concomitant lessened functionality, compared with twelve months post-stroke status. Call me a worry wart, but I was sufficiently concerned that I scheduled a visit with neurologist in Asheville, North Carolina. He seemed to minimize the notion of stroke progression and likened my observations to a person who might be comparing pre-stroke functionality with present limitations.

However, he suggested consultation with a physical therapist, which occurred at Pardee Physical Therapy in Hendersonville, North Carolina, with Chloe Egan, therapist, in late March 2009.

Within a few minutes, Chloe noted that the sensorial changes occurring in both the arm and leg were consistent with inadvertent

1   Lacunar: Lacunar stroke or lacunar infarct (LACI) is a type of stroke that results from occlusion of one of the penetrating arteries that provides blood to the brain's deep structures.

pressure on nerves associated with cervical and lumbar vertebrae. The cervical nerve dysfunction she could associate with my walking posture; she noted that my head led my torso, as I had assumed a forward bend while walking. Similarly, she noted that long hours sitting at the computer while producing this manuscript were again associated with poor posture, as I tend to slide forward on my chair, putting pressure on the lumbar nerves mentioned. Below is my summary of the first PT session.

Summary of Physical Therapy Observations

Chloe was very perceptive and immediately focused on my posture as the possible etiology of what I considered regressive hemi-paretic stroke issues, which manifest as increased numbness in the left hand, arm, and foot with attendant less mobility. She noted the following:

WHILE SITTING

- I tend to sit with upper body tilted to the right, resulting in a structural angle that causes the right knee to be advanced in front of the left.
- This also results in leg nerve distortion as well as left arm nerve distortion, exacerbating numbness.
- I tend to slouch, sliding my rump forward in the chair, putting uneven pressure on the low back muscles, which can contribute to low back muscle discomfort.

WHILE STANDING

- Right rib cage is twisted, giving the appearance of being in front of the left side.
- This also causes the shoulder blade to wing out significantly.
- Right shoulder is not level with the left, nor is right hip level with the left.
- Arms do not hang freely or swing adequately.
- Head leans ahead of the torso, with the chin protruding, putting stress on neck muscle and nerve function.

- I put more weight on the right than on the left side of my body.

WHILE WALKING

- My left stride is much shorter than my right, and as mentioned, my arms do not hang freely or swing as desired.
- Heels do not strike first, and shoes are not suitable.

IN GENERAL

- I do not make the left side do its share of work, which results in a contorted posture.
- What I consider regressive stroke issues are more likely effects that are posture-related.
- I need to move more while being more conscious of postures at the computer and everywhere else.
- I can use walking sticks to help regain gait performance, but I need more downward pressure on the sticks and need to concentrate on longer and more rapid strides.
- Progress in gait and recovery in general will be directly related to my level of desire and willingness to do the work necessary to make the corrections.
- This is a critical time to address my issues; otherwise regressive changes will accelerate, leaving no chance for recovery.

In my judgment, these observations by Chloe are pivotal to my ultimate version of stroke recovery. I believe Chloe is indeed a gifted therapist, and with her long history in stroke management, I learned more from her in five minutes than in all my other PT combined. Actually reviewing her comments while finishing this manuscript was very helpful, as my push to finish required even longer hours at the computer with significantly more associated neuropathy.

An Advocate Is A Needed Friend

Every health care professional who has a special knowledge, skill, or training related to a particular disease or condition should be given an opportunity to augment his or her income by registering as a health care advocate. This would be useful for patients facing a problem within their area of knowledge and who would pay for counsel regarding the best facility and medical service within a fifty-mile radius.

As an example, having a stroke in a small town in western North Carolina, I did not know there was even such a thing as a stroke center, let alone that one existed a few miles away in Asheville. Certainly, no one at our local hospital ever mentioned it, and I guess it is possible that since my stroke was considered mild, no one felt it was conceivable that I would want or need specialized care. Had there been a stroke advocate I could have hired at the time, very likely much of my anxiety and stress could have been avoided. This is a service I gladly would have paid out of pocket, just for stroke-related advice on what to expect and where to go for expert counsel.

I did make a valiant effort to meet with one at Duke University in December of 2008, all to no avail, as they rescheduled my appointment five times with the hope that it did not inconvenience me. I finally gave up.

Medical Solutions Of Last Resort

The standard catalogue of treatment for medical problems is typically confined to the diseases for which clinical studies have been done that meet the criteria for establishing medical fact. These types of study usually involve double-blind placebo-controlled patient observations where specific laboratory tests are available to provide proof of association of symptom and cure of any given malady. While this is the accepted approach demanded by conventional science, it fails to give any consideration to the numerous medical problems where clinicians have discovered cause and treatments that, though effective, have not been supported by controlled studies that prove validity.

The firsthand clinical experience that may have been accumulating since biblical times lies dormant and often ignored, even though once rediscovered, it can provide useful and even critical medical knowledge. As we have now moved into the age of the Internet, where everyone is on an equal footing to gather and assess medical solutions to intractable problems, the only ingredient missing from trying clinical but not sanctioned solutions seems to be related to the straitjacket into which organizations such as the AMA have placed their members. Anyone who dares to stray from the clearly marked approved path risks the wrath of colleagues and peers, funding for grants, and all of the other privileges granted to those who stay in the box while practicing medicine.

What I think should happen is for our publically funded research institutions, or more likely the force of the Bill Gates Foundation, to sponsor the creation of a searchable journal of anecdotal medical findings. This is where clinicians could submit evidence of their clinical experience focused on strategies that they have found will work but is not necessarily supported by controlled evidence. They should be able to offer without penalty whatever irrefutable evidence they think they have that could represent unconsidered solutions or solutions of last resort. Since creating and maintaining such a record would far exceed the resources of any one person, this must be a product of a dedicated staff of funded scientists.

My goal is to encourage thinking in this direction and try to figure out the best way to provide the public with the tools needed to recover anecdotal evidence of medical successes. I think such a medical search tool eventually would rival Google and PubMed in terms of contributions that lead to medical progress.

It seems to me that medical regulatory authorities should be able to accommodate functional treatment strategies, as long as supporting clinical experience is sufficiently persuasive to show no harmful effects, and as long as the patient does not expect insurance agencies to finance their treatment of last resort. What we are talking about here is providing a tool for the public to systematically search for any anecdotal avenue that might lead to hope for those left with no hope.

Those who are in charge of your health, starting mostly with *you,* along with your doctor, must get past an ego-sensitive resource with which most folks fail to consort. Let me give you some background.

We all have a little trouble adjusting to the new boundaries of medical science that now include the true energetic nature of our being. This new dimension is beautifully characterized in the book by Gary Zukav called *The Dancing Wu Li Masters.* You need only read through Chapter One to grasp the entire message. If you get to Chapter Two, you have gone too far. In his book, we are characterized as "patterns of organic energy." Our perception of substance, according to quantum physics, is actually an illusion. We consist of nothing but patterns of energy. The closest thing we can come to in defining ourselves as of substance is to first decide what we think we are looking at. If we think we look like a particle of energy, then we will appear in that context. If we think we look like a wave of energy, we will appear in *that* context, as previously mentioned. We know, for example, that an electron cannot be measured.

We thus are really essentially patterns of nothingness. Let me give you two "concrete" examples.

Get out your chemistry book and look at the periodic table of elements. Notice the three most important elements composing all forms of life. The atomic numbers of these three are: carbon (6), nitrogen (7), and oxygen (8). Notice that if you add one electron to the nitrogen atom, you suddenly have an atom of oxygen. If you take away an electron from nitrogen, you suddenly have an atom of carbon. How can this be that you can add or take away a unit of nothingness and yet change everything?

Here is another example: look at platinum (78), gold (79), and mercury (80). Go figure.

Finally you have the necessary background to get to my message. We have unexplained (idiopathic) diseases mostly because we are not fully prepared to look over the walls of conventional medicine into the realm of holistic medicine. Let me repeat: those who are skilled in energy therapy (esoteric energy) are able to sense the etheric patterns of energy surrounding each of us. With that skill, they can sense energy imbalances and restore them.

This sounds like a panacea, but it is not. First of all, while a holistic physician can have good insight on a possible health-management strategy, there are licensing and peer boundaries that make it difficult or even impossible to freely prescribe holistic remedies. The most they can do, as I understand the problem, is to let the patient know of a possible path and then leave it to the patient to decide whether to take that path on his or her own. Obviously this requires a patient with significant health savvy. Too bad but true, it seems.

LESSON TWELVE

Final Lesson

For the final lesson, I have listed in order of importance all of the chemical and physical strategies I evaluated that positively and unequivocally proved to be beneficial for my stroke recovery process. "_____"

Final Exam

Okay, fellow students of stroke, as you complete this course, I as teacher's pet have been asked to issue one last assignment as you move on toward your next life lesson. The assignment is for you to read the book *MIND POWER into the 21st Century* by John Kehoe, a number-one world bestseller. Pay particular attention to Chapter Eight on intuition where he notes the paths of numerous historic figures who attributed success to their trust in intuition. To repeat for emphasis, his examples include Mozart, Socrates, Einstein, Edison, Marconi, Henry Ford, Luther Burbank, Madame Curie, and "Nobel Laureates by the bundle" who have attributed their success directly to their intuition. He goes on to quote Henry Mintzberg from the *Harvard Review* regarding a study of high-ranking corporate executives who were "constantly relying on hunches to cope with problems too complex for rational thinking". He concluded, ***"Success does not lie in that narrow-minded concept called rationality, it lies in a blend of clear headed logic and powerful intuition"***. (Emphasis mine.)

Within your review of this course, in preparation for your final exam, you will want to:

1. Review the list of stroke and heart attack risk factors currently recognized by the NIH, the American Heart Association, and the American Stroke Association. Note the conspicuous absence of any mention of dehydration.

2. Do not expect to pass this course—or live as long as you might—if you cannot answer the questions in the box below.

TABLE #3: FINAL EXAM	
QUESTION	**ANSWER**
What three blood features are common throughout the world, among those who live to be 100 or more and which of them is the most important?	Low sugar Low triglycerides Low insulin Low insulin is the most important.
Name the health features that are associated with blood clotting, and thus to heart attack and stroke.	Dehydration Metabolic syndrome Hemeagglutinating-type bacterial and viral infections such as influenza Magnesium deficiency Fibrinogen level Stress Hormones
What are the most important things we can do to minimize heart attack and stroke risk besides diet?	Daily exercise, lower blood pressure, and drink more water.
What time of day do most strokes occur, and why?	Before noon, because water is extracted from our tissues during the night, and excreted upon awakening, resulting in maximal point of dehydration, and best chance for clots to form.
What time of day do most heart attacks occur and why?	Precisely the same response and reasoning as for strokes.

General Observations

If we choose a low-energy life, we are more focused on self-gratification, what we can get rather than what we can give. We are attracted to drugs, dogma, and other vehicles of escape. Be mindful of the words of Einstein: "foolish faith in authority is the worst enemy of truth."

If we choose to live at a higher level of life energy, we are more focused on caring for others, compassion, forgiveness, and gratitude. These energy descriptions have been gathered from the writings of some of the great minds.

So where does this leave us in the healing process? Well, since in my opinion, we live in a perfect universe, whatever methods we use to achieve health will be precisely what is needed for our evolution. Thus, if we try a given treatment modality that does not seem to lead us through the path of our intention, we simply must accept the reality that our intention was not of sufficient cosmic dimension that we can know what is really best for us and thus cannot be questioned. But do keep in mind the final prescient words of Richard Bach in his book, *Illusions,* to which I subscribe, which were …

Everything

In this book

May be

Wrong.

Was it a particle, or was it a wave?

Was it a god, or was it a devil?

EPILOGUE

For those of us on the outside looking in, it is easy to get the impression that the funding arm of NIH is faced with a dilemma. They try to accommodate first-line scientists who need funding for basic research and then balance that demand with scientists representing private enterprise, wanting support for drug evaluation. Enter into this mix an unsponsored idea, the merit of which requires faith and common sense, and it would find no likely chance of audience with NIH.

Take the general thesis of this book, for example, or more importantly, the work of Batmanghelidj in his book, *You Are Not Sick, You Are Thirsty.* I think it is fair to predict that the subject of doing a study of water-consumption impact on heart attack, stroke and all other dehydration-related maladies would be excluded from any consideration.

From a common-sense perspective, the subject is way too obvious to satisfy the intellectual challenge of developing complex biochemical pathways to explain the impact of dehydration. To suggest a non-pharmaceutical remedy for heart attack (HA), stroke (S), diabetes (D), Alzheimer's (AD), obesity (O), and all of the other possible dehydration-associated diseases mentioned by Batmanghelidj, simply comparing cohorts with and without adequate hydration is probably way beneath the dignity of serious scientists.

In defense of a common-sense approach to funding decisions and to test credulity, how in the world can the scientific community continue to ignore the facts that both heart attack and stroke occur most often before noon, while dismissing the notion that dehydration and stress hormones are reasonable co-factors? Beyond that diatribe, here is a strategy that anyone can use immediately to try to minimize stroke, heart attack, and all other dehydration-associated health issues.

If you think what I have covered in this book makes sense, you need not wait for the research world to sanction increased water consumption. Just consider the following:

1. As it now stands, most people arise in the morning, void their bladder, and drink a jolt or two of coffee—itself a dehydrating agent. They get themselves to work and start coping with the stress du jour.

2. Here is a better idea: Arise early, immediately drink a glass or two of warm or hot water to compensate for nighttime dehydration. You will find it is a satisfying practice, giving you the feeling that you have done something positive to help prevent a heart attack or stroke for that day.

3. Make a point to at least try to consume the recommended water intake during the day, which is to divide your weight by two and then consume that number in ounces of water each day.

Let's get real; hardly anyone will drink that amount of water when not thirsty. So here is what we must do. Fill a Brita jug or the like with water and leave it in sight all day (on every desk in every office there should be one) as a reminder to drink a glass or at least a half glass of water. Other fluids do not count, and room-temperature or warmer water is best, but cold water is certainly okay. Even a sip is still more than you would have consumed otherwise. And make a special effort to insist on giving the elderly or incapacitated plenty of water, especially AD members of family.

What to Do if You Have Already Had a Warning Stroke

1. The critical first step is to get your blood pressure under control. Try to get it into the 120/70 range with medication and rehydration as soon as possible.

2. Understand a bit more about BP management; realize that there are numerous classes of BP management drugs as follows:

Blood Pressure Management Drugs

ACE inhibitors
Alpha-blockers
Angiotensin II receptor blockers
Beta-blockers
Blood vessel dilators or vasodilators
Calcium channel-blockers
Central agonists
Combined alpha and beta-blockers
Diuretics
Peripheral adrenergic inhibitors
Sympathetic nerve inhibitors

In my experience, you should recognize that the likelihood of anyone knowing which class of drug will work for you is marginal. It seems to me that it became a matter of trial and error to finally find the class of drug that worked for me. I went through both the alpha- and beta-blockers, as well as ACE inhibitors, before we finally found that Norvasc, a calcium channel-blocker worked reliably for me. That took about two years to figure out. Inexcusable, I say.

3. It seems to me that BP management should be a three-step process:

a) You and your doctor should immediately do a dedicated survey to figure out which drug class will work for you, if you do not already know.

b) With that information in hand, in my opinion you should consider combining that drug with selected nutrients/supplements known to reduce BP. Supplements I've come across that are said to reduce BP include vitamin E, taurine, ample magnesium, acetyl carnitine, carnitine, Nattokinase, and Arginine.

c) Once you have a stable and predictable BP record, consider having your doctor start weaning you off the prescription drug and get to the point where the combination of adequate hydration, with supplements and diet, can hold your pressure in the desired range. Ditch the meds if possible, and rely on natural solutions.

One thing is for sure: unless there is some other compelling medical reason that demands a diuretic class of BP medication, use caution in using that drug class, since it is precisely dehydration that got us into trouble in the first place. Feel free to remind your doctor of that point of view.

Let me return to the blood-pressure story before leaving this scene. I think there is much more information to be gleaned from BP measurements. It seems to me that what is really important is a measurement of the total workload placed on the heart. Maybe a useful indicator would be to calculate the product of the diastolic, the systolic, and the heart rate, to possibly indicate a theoretical arbitrarily derived unit of total workload. When I constructed such a nomogram, I found that low heart rate appeared to compensate significantly for elevated BP in terms of total workload. A high heart rate put the numbers off the chart. I got the impression that we are missing important data by ignoring heart rate as related to BP.

While pontificating, let me also point out the peculiar conundrum related to the use of statin drugs. We are cautioned about consuming grapefruit juice while using statins, as that fruit seems to potentiate the drug activity. I should think that is actually good news, since it implies that we should be able to titrate grapefruit up while titrating statin dose down, to find the lowest possible statin dose level needed, which hopefully when combined with adequate hydration would allow us to ditch another drug eventually. I do not think anyone ever died from a deficiency of aspirin, statin drug, or the like. Think about it.

I hope you did not miss the discussion of stroke mechanisms involving influenza virus, where it was shown that influenza infection was associated with increased stroke risk and those vaccinated, with reduced risk. It seems to me there is a double potential benefit from flu vaccination. Actually, in my opinion, the benefit may be even greater, as I believe anything that stimulates our immune system periodically is beneficial.

A Tip for Primary Care Physicians

We all appreciate it when doctors are cost-conscious about their advice. However, I think that within that effort, sometimes we are short-changed if the physician makes recommendations that are cost-based or insurance-driven, rather than on what is really needed for the patient if cost was no object. In other words, I think it would be helpful if physicians would voluntarily first tell their patients what they would do, or would have done, if they faced the issue themselves. Please don't wait for the patient to ask, as most of us assume that the recommendations made under insurance provisions are the final word, and that clearly is not the case.

Please, let the patients decide if they want to spend the money out of pocket for a strategy not covered by insurance. You might be surprised to find that those who can afford the best advice are more than willing to pay for it out of pocket.

ADDENDUM

To reflect the strength of the arm of dehydration in disease processes, I am including this addendum, which is really a testimony to the work of Batmanghelidj. Given the power of the possibilities already outlined with stroke and heart attack, I can see where the third of the world's three top killers should be brought into brighter light in the context of dehydration.

The Dehydration Cancer Connection

My search for a dehydration-cancer connection is a back-door approach by first looking for possible cancer-stroke relationships. Since there seems to be a reasonable connection between stroke and dehydration already made herein, the frequency of stroke reported among cancer subjects should be a reasonable index of a true dehydration-cancer relationship. While it is not my goal to produce a comprehensive review of the subject, there is a wealth of study associating many cancers with stroke events. A few of these are offered as representative studies.

The Cancer-Stroke Connection

It turns out that there is a substantial association between stroke and most forms of cancer. For example, quoting from their paper, "Stroke and Cancer: A Review," by Griswold, W., Oberndorfer, S., and Struhal W. (2009): "Stroke is a disabling disease, and can add to the burden of patients already suffering from cancer. Several mechanisms of stroke exist in cancer patients, which can be directly tumor related, because of coagulation disorders, infections, and therapy related." They go on to state, "Stroke can also occur as the first sign of cancer, or lead to its detection." They note that, "The classical literature suggests that stroke occurs more frequently in cancer patients than in the normal population." They further state, "More recent studies report a very similar incidence between cancer and non-cancer patients."

As written by Teri Nguyen and Lisa M. DeAngelis (2006) of Sloane-Kettering: "Cancer patients are at increased risk for stroke from direct and indirect effects of their malignancy. Some tumors are at high risk for cerebrovascular complications. Certain stroke mechanisms are specific to cancer, such as compression and occlusion of cerebral vessels by tumor, coagulopathy predisposing to hemorrhage and thrombosis, and treatment-related atherosclerosis."

To gain some perspective on the problem, it is informative to notice the list of the common cancer types that are diagnosed with the greatest frequency in United States.

This information is a product of the National Cancer Institute, as captured from the American Cancer Society and other sources. They state, "The most common type of cancer on the list is non-melanoma skin cancer which represents about half of all cancer diagnosed in this country. The cancer on the list with the lowest incidence is thyroid cancer."

TABLE #4: Cancer List
Bladder
Breast
Colorectal
Endometrial
Kidney
Leukemia
Lung
Melanoma
Non-Hodgkin Lymphoma
Non-Melanoma skin cancer
Pancreatic
Thyroid cancer

It is clear that the relationship between cancer and stroke is well-documented, and thus, according to my working thesis, a significant role for dehydration can be inferred. As peripheral support for the dehydration connection, we can refer to the papers by Charlene Laino (2009) entitled "Albuminuria Strongly Associated with Stroke Risk", and in "Association of Albuminuria and Cancer Incidence" by Lone Jorgensen, et al., (2008).

The medical definition of albuminuria includes the notation that it may occur with high fever and dehydration. Although not found within cancer literature that I viewed, it seems entirely feasible, given that a magnesium deficiency is shown to be a major player in the dehydration/stroke picture, and that a magnesium deficit, as discussed in the stroke/insulin resistance sections is a powerful factor in clot formation leading to stroke and heart attack. It is not a big jump for the need to look more carefully for a magnesium role in the cancer-stroke problem.

Whatever the final determination of cancer-stroke mechanisms, it seems clear—especially for those with the dual challenge of cancer and stroke—that both for prevention and for management, there should be a strong component of care that includes rigorous attention to hydration.

General Observations

As I have slogged my way through the murky history of stroke research, I am left with the impression that our health state of affairs in terms of dehydration and insulin resistance is hair-raising. The potential for damage to health worldwide is so enormous that, in my opinion, a full investigation of the breadth and depth of the potential impact of dehydration and insulin resistance on other diseases should become first-priority research, done on an emergency basis.

Investing most of our research dollars on the most visible targets, such as cancer? Sure, that is important, but underneath, let's not overlook the obvious, even if it is not revenue-attractive or designed to keep pharmaceutical firms and doctors busy.

Breaking the Barriers of Science

In his book *Vibrational Medicine*, published in 1988 by Bear & CO of Santa Fe, NM, Richard Gerber MD, accurately points out the difficulty of publishing any new health–related article where the subject has no published history. He observes correctly that a Catch-22 is operative since if a controversial subject has never been accepted by a medical journal, it becomes impossible to present data to support the idea because every medical journal must rely upon previous references to such work to give the new idea credibility. Gerber has nevertheless found his voice through his book *Vibrational Medicine,* demonstrating that as a result of this "rule of science" medical progress will be limited.

Within the text, I presented a rather elaborate diagram, showing why atrial fibrillation—a common feature of heart attack and stroke—is a symptom, rather than a cause. I believe this type of reasoning could be a useful approach for distinguishing between symptoms and cause for many disease processes and their management. Here are some thoughts along that line:

- I believe fever is a good example of a problem that is typically approached by trying to manage the symptom, rather than the cause.
- I believe Alzheimer's disease is another wasteful example of treating the symptoms before having any solid notion of cause.
- I believe that manifestation of cancer is a symptom of an unrecognized metabolic problem.
- I believe that high blood pressure, as the number one purported risk factor for heart attack and stroke, is clearly a symptom but not a cause.
- I believe there are some common features that contribute to the diseases stated, as well as many other diseases; these features include dehydration, magnesium deficiency, and excess stress hormones.

Our national fixation on treating symptoms as the first line of attack while forfeiting cause will keep us safely hidden in the dark ages of medicine.

APPENDIX I

Helpful Drugs For Recovery

Drugs Said to Be Helpful for Stroke Recovery

It must be pretty obvious that if there were such a thing as a drug that is helpful for stroke recovery, it would be widely known and used. Since there is no such candidate, I looked at the anecdotal reports and came across one drug that sounded interesting enough that I decided to evaluate it as follows.

Deprenyl (selegiline)

When you Google the terms *deprenyl* and *stroke,* you will uncover 28,000 entries for what seems to be a most remarkable drug. Not only is it said to extend life, but it is also described as facilitating recovery after stroke. You will find woven into its history a time when it was in and then out of favor when prescribed for Parkinson's disease. The popular drug rebel, Dr. Julian Whitaker, describes deprenyl as "what good pharmaceuticals are all about," and seems to promote its use in certain circumstances. With support from my doctor, I tried the drug, with great expectations. However, before you do, you should know about side effects, and before that, something about how it works.

Requiring biochemical neurotransmitters, the brain has a mechanism to remove a specific neurotransmitter once it has done its job, and that is where two types of monoamine oxidase (MAO A, and B) come into play. Deprenyl can irreversibly knock out MAO enzymes, leaving the excess of certain neurotransmitters (dopamine, histamine, and tyramine for example) to continue doing their thing, which is most undesirable. Dopamine is associated with the Parkinson's disease syndrome, while tyramine is associated with aged-cheese or dried-fruit effect. For those who are especially sensitive, as am I, the effect of excess histamine or tyramine manifests as a persistent headache and rapidly elevated blood pressure among other things. The half-life of Deprenyl ranges from four days for residence in the majority of the body (to deal with MAO-A), with up to forty days' residence time in the brain (to deal with MAO-B). So once you knock out your MAO protective enzymes, all one can do is wait for the body to wash out the remaining Deprenyl using a carefully managed diet to minimize intake of high monoamine foods. I concluded the price was too high to fool around with it beyond my initial evaluation period. Of course, there was no way to know if it had any potential for facilitating my stroke recovery, and I was not interested enough to pursue it. If you are already prone to cheese or dry-fruit headaches, then without question forget Deprenyl; it is not for amateur health management. There is just too much potential for lasting damage with continued use of such a powerful enzyme inhibitor. Best advice: do the search routine and check it out for yourself if I have not convinced you.

I came across another substance sold through health-food stores with fascinating claims. This agent is called Nattokinase, which is an enzyme extracted from a soy food product called natto, long used by the Japanese as a folk remedy for heart and vascular diseases. Some of the claims include: cure for stroke, cure for blood clots, supports longevity, and improves circulation. You may want to study Nattokinase for purported benefits and for risks. It has been proposed as a replacement for the blood thinner Coumadin; however as far as I can determine, no substantial studies have been done to justify its use for that purpose. Like so many other proposed products, the best advice is to find out if the product is being used by any stroke center—they will be the first to welcome a legitimate addition to their stroke armament. Do not become beguiled by print advertising. There seem to be no rules or conscience associated with claims made. I make note of this product so that if it eventually can be shown unequivocally capable of passing through the gut while retaining its fibrinolytic property, there may well be a place for it in modern medicine. My doctor and I, in fact, carefully titrated it as a partial replacement for Coumadin. However, we were unable to reach a definitive conclusion, so I decided not to pursue it further, relying on Coumadin to provide blood thinning for clot protection. Having experienced a stroke, which I associated with unwise withdrawal of Coumadin, I have utmost respect for a proven approach to clot prevention, and Nattokinase is more directed toward clot (fibrinolytic) dissolution than prevention.

The upshot of this area of study is there is no such thing as a drug to affect stroke recovery that I could find. I will point out, however, that vinpocetine and hyperizine are described in stroke and AD literature as being helpful for memory issues, both of which easily can be studied if interested.

Literature Research Tools

The advent of literature search tools such as PubMed and Google has led to revolutionary access and recovery of medical history, and in my opinion, probably are the most significant early contributions to the world of medical research ever. Both made their appearance around 1996.

History of Google

Google began in January of 1996. Naturally I Googled "Google history"—to uncover this information.

History of PubMed

PubMed was first released in January 1996 and served as a portal to MEDLINE in 1997 (National Library of Medicine biomedical database).

There are dozens of additional medical search engines that I have not explored but are easily found in a Google search using the term: *medical search engines.* Another useful engine is Cochrane.

The point I am trying to make is that the shortest and quickest route to any serious investigation of medical issues and medical history is through the enormous power of the Internet. The big trick is to be able to distinguish factual data from fiction-laced advertising. There often seems to be no moral guidance as to what one can present as factual medical information on some websites, so the word is ***caution.***

The importance of Internet searches, for example, cannot be overstated; they are pivotal. Thus, mission one in looking for health-related answers is to have access to a computer and learn how to use the Internet effectively. By that I mean learn by experience what terms or strings of terms will give you the most direct path to your subject search.

I marvel at the power of this tool every time I use it. For my purposes, I usually print out a copy of the first Google or PubMed search page and then scan individual entries, finally selecting what seems to be the most relevant. Then I usually print a copy of those entries for later reference.

As a cautionary note: Google is an advertising medium, and thus many entries are articles that may be biased toward the sale of a product. The information may not be factual, so caution is urged. This is not the case with PubMed articles, for example, as no advertising is seen, in my experience, and you can rely on the authenticity of articles quoted.

The power of Google has not been overlooked in the daily practice of medicine, as I came across one doctor who keeps the Google screen on all day in his office so he can quickly reference any question he may have relative to his daily work. I was impressed.

You will find that Internet searches are compelling. While preparing this manuscript, for example, it was not unusual for me to go to the computer in the middle of the night for a question that just could not wait for morning. You will find that the searches may be endless, because one search can lead to numerous forks in the road of thought. Anyone who wants to take charge of his or her own health decisions must have computer access.

How Medicare Could Save Money

1. Patient Evaluation of Health Care Workers
   To reduce fraud and incompetency, it seems to me that patients should be given the opportunity to make an annual assessment of their providers of care and verify that the service was actually rendered. This could be a simple rating of acceptable or unacceptable. If more than 50 percent of respondents judged their provider as unacceptable, then that person should be enjoined from further Medicare funding. If more than 90 percent of responders found the provider acceptable or better, then that finding also should be made public. The patient should receive notification of how much Medicare paid their care provider annually.

2. Patient Evaluation of Health Care Facility/Services
   Similar to the suggestion above, patients should be advised of the annual cost paid for them by Medicare. For example, a patient receiving physical therapy should be able to rate the facility, where again if more than 50 percent of respondents judged the service as inadequate, that facility should be enjoined from receiving future Medicare funding.

3. Medical procedures and drugs not supported by data showing a published statistical advantage on life expectancy should not be supported by Medicare funding. Medical

professionals not holding a current license should be clearly identified.

4. Medical procedures found anecdotally useful but not sanctioned by Medicare should be the subject to a periodic test of opinion (common sense) from the medical community, overriding Medicare judgment where indicated. A case to be tested would be hyperbaric oxygen treatment (HBOT) for heart attack and stroke, in my opinion. For heaven's sake, at least do a five-year trial evaluation and compare mortality and medical costs.

5. <u>Medicare Payment to Pharmaceutical Companies to Justify Use of Their Drug:</u> A case in point is where those who use statin drugs are required to have "simple blood tests" done, to determine if there is any evidence of liver damage. Please tell us why the American public should pay for laboratory tests to prove safety of the drug, when clearly that should be the responsibility of the manufacturer. Their drugs either are safe and effective or they are not.

It is obvious that this arrangement needs a fresh look. If drug firms want the data, they should pay for it—not the patient or insurance. As it stands now, I have no idea how the facts surrounding drug performance reach the public. We are most certainly entitled to the accumulated unfiltered data, since we are paying for those "simple blood tests".

6. <u>Medicare Payment for Unjustified Equipment:</u> Heaven only knows how deep this problem runs. But let me give you one example: there is a frequent ad on television (obviously never seen by Medicare management), encouraging us to get an electric scooter. So sure are they that Medicare will pay for it, they will give you one free if Medicare does not pay. An acquaintance, who knows a freebee when she sees one, arranged for her mother to receive one of the famous scooters. And guess what—her mother lives in a modular

home so small the cart cannot get through the doorways, so
it has never been used. Even Ripley would be impressed.

7. Need for Standardized ER Stroke Evaluation
   Since you may never have gone through the ER stroke
   routine, you might not know what goes on. I have, and
   I must tell you.

I get to the ER at a Florida hospital, tell the admitting person I
have a problem with my gait, and she tells me to return to the busy
waiting room and she will call me. After fifteen minutes, I return to
the desk and tell her I think I have stroke symptoms. I am whisked
into the ER for CAT and MRI scans, where I remain for the next three
hours and where there was no intervention attempted whatsoever of
any kind—nothing! Now, even I have come to know that this is an
oxygen emergency for brain tissue, and that all effort should be made
to minimize brain swelling and progression of symptoms.

The point I want to make is that we *must* have a standardized
protocol for ER heart/stroke management—or no Medicare funding.
It also would be most helpful if the person at the admitting desk was
familiar with heart/stroke symptoms.

8. There should be a system to weed out frivolous prescriptions
   issued by health care workers.

9. Hospitals with higher-than-average infection rates should be
   on probation for one year, with Medicare funding suspended.
   And most certainly they should be publicly identified.

10. Give us the facts: Why not place some responsibility for
    Medicare or Medicaid expenditure with the patient? As
    things stand right now, anyone can go to their primary care
    physician and request and receive treatments for ailments
    ranging from casual to serious. Some subjects use this
    service simply to get attention, often faking symptoms.
    Why should we not have the facts that tell each Medicare/
    Medicaid-eligible citizen exactly what his or her lifetime

statistical dollar share is of the health care pie and how much has been expended?

Once we each had some notion of how much each recipient has already consumed in care costs, we would know how much money is allocated for the balance of our lives. With an annual account statement in hand, we each could carefully decide if our current symptom du jour is really worth the charge to our health account. At the very least, we could try this idea for five years and see what happens to cost and patient service numbers. I think those who are able and willing to think will realize that they need to conserve as much of their health care account as possible to have resources to meet possible devastating illnesses in later years.

While I'm at it, here is another pet peeve—why in the world can patients not receive a gown that has front closure? Are we hospitalized for the convenience of the doctor or for the patient? We ought to at least get that much straight. And here is one more. What possible value is there for a nurse to weigh a patient with each visit? The weight of our clothing varies so greatly that any recorded number other than "shower weight" is meaningless. One thing they could do to be useful would be a temperature recording, as small consistent variations in body temperature can signal significant hormonal changes. I get the impression that weight and BP readings must be necessary to constitute an official Medicare visit—just a guess. With obesity and diabetes rampant, why don't doctors regularly monitor A1C values as part of physical routine? My thought is that it must boil down to a Medicare decision—just a guess. Physicians must have a boatload of suggestions to repair Medicare/Medicaid. Anyone ever thought to ask them?

Results of all clinical observations should be electronically recorded for proof of performance and recoverability. All entries should be tagged with a social security number for historical tracking.

APPENDIX IV

Nutrients And Supplements

Following are examples of agents described as being useful for stroke recovery.

I cannot certify that any of them have a proven record for stroke help. However, I present them with a summary of claims made and leave it up to the reader to decide if any of them make enough sense to give them a try. The big problem, of course, is that there is no way to prove whether anything you try was really effective, since you cannot know how your recovery would have played out if you had not taken the agent.

Doctors with whom I have had contact offered no suggestions whatsoever, so it came down to my search of the literature, choosing to try to help myself, rather than doing nothing.

Acetyl Carnitine (ALCAR)

This material is a product of the combination of carnitine and acetic acid. It is synthesized in our bodies from the amino acids lysine and methionine, and thus natural to us.

Claims:
- Is an antioxidant
- Improves peripheral neuropathy and peripheral nerve regeneration
- Slows Alzheimer's Disease
- Improves mental functioning
- Slows effects of aging on brain functions

- Helps regenerate neurons damaged by free radicals
- Crosses blood-brain barrier
- Beneficial for carnitine deficiency
- Wards off senile dementia
- Helpful in Parkinson's and diabetes
- Improves cerebrovascular efficiency in the elderly
- Often used in combination with CoQ10 and lipoic acid
- Little or no side effects
- Promotes synthesis of acetyl choline, a neurotransmitter
- Prevents loss of nerve function
- Facilitates transport of fatty acids into mitochondria
- Useful in treatment of drug-induced peripheral neuropathy
- Enhances cellular energy production
- Reduces advanced glycation end products (AGEs)
- Suppresses ventricular arrhythmia

Arginine

Arginine is an amino acid in a class by itself, since it is made by the body; thus it is not considered an essential amino acid. Yet it seems not to be in sufficient supply to meet all needs and has consequently earned the classification of semi essential.

Claims:
- Antioxidant, anti-aging, anti-cancer
- Lowers LDL cholesterol, homocysteine
- Lowers blood pressure
- Increases nitric oxide, muscle mass, thymus activity, blood circulation
- Reduces risk of heart disease
- Improves healing time following tissue injury
- Enhances male sexual health
- Promotes healing of hemorrhoids

- Performance-enhancing
- Improves blood vessel elasticity
- Improves circulatory, immune, and nerve system
- Helps prevent heart attack and stroke
- Relaxes blood vessels by contributing to the production of nitric oxide; almost every benefit claimed for arginine is really a claim for nitric oxide, an enzyme mediated product of arginine.

Disadvantages:
- May activate latent viruses such as herpes simplex
- May have adverse effect following heart attack
- May worsen asthma and lung inflammation (conflicting reports, however)
- May worsen schizophrenia

Arginine, when not in perfect balance with lysine, is associated with activation of latent herpes virus. This condition exists in about 20 percent of the population; this is the family of viruses that can cause cold sores, chicken pox, genital herpes, and shingles. Turning this information around suggests that outbreaks of those conditions can be ameliorated by increasing lysine intake (works for me).

Alpha Lipoic Acid, also Known as Thiotic Acid

Lipoic Acid (RLA) is one of the most important new nutraceutical compounds to hit the market. It is a powerful antioxidant, a critical co-factor in ATP production.

Claims:
- Powerful antioxidant
- Re-activates other antioxidants such as vitamins C and E, and helps maintain levels of glutathione
- Supports memory, mood, mental clarity, concentration, and alertness
- Proven benefit in diabetic neuropathy

- A study was funded by NIH for possible benefit in Alzheimer's patients, but no results could be found
- Often used with acetyl carnitine; in fact, if you compare claims for both agents, they are almost identical
- Shows benefit in slowing progression of diabetic kidney disease
- Improves insulin sensitivity
- Helps control blood sugar
- Helps eliminate free radicals
- May help protect from atherosclerosis and inflammation of blood vessels
- May help protect against stroke

Magnesium

Magnesium is a major mineral that you get from your diet that is important for many biochemical functions, and found in nuts, seeds, whole grains, and legumes.

Opinion for free: This is probably the most important supplement you can take for vascular diseases.

Claims: Severe arrhythmias may occur as a result of magnesium deficiency.

Magnesium may:
- Reduce incidence of tachycardia in heart disease patients
- Prevent atherosclerosis
- Inhibit abnormal blood clotting by reducing platelet adhesiveness
- Exert antispasmodic effects on blood vessels
- Improve heart function in cardiomyopathy patients
- Dilate cerebral arteries and improve cerebral blood flow
- Alleviate congestive heart failure

- Lower diastolic and systolic blood pressure in hypertensive patients
- Alleviate many causes of intermittent claudication
- Treat and prevent ischemic heart disease
- Alleviate some types of angina
- Help prevent heart attack and reduce chance of death following heart attack
- Provide significant protection against strokes, by minimizing vascular spasms
- Reduce after-effects of stroke when administered by infusion within six hours of stroke
- Modulate electrical potential of cell membranes
- Strengthen bladder muscles—(incontinence)
- Prevent re-appearance of kidney stones
- Alleviate dry eyes
- Lower cholesterol
- Increase HDL and lower LDL and triglycerides
- Facilitate weight loss in the obese
- Improve electrical nerve impulses at nerve-muscle junctions
- Realize that magnesium depletion is a product of aging and recognize that 59 percent of AIDS patients are found to be magnesium deficient

Taurine

A conditionally essential amino acid made by the body from amino acids methionine and cysteine.

Claims:

- An unbound amino acid not involved in protein synthesis, said to be the most abundant amino acid in the body
- Useful for atherosclerosis, heart disorders, cardiovascular issues, congestive heart failure, arrhythmias, hypertension, reduces platelet stickiness

- Associated with edema and epilepsy
- Lowers cholesterol
- Stroke prevention, lowers blood pressure
- Taurine with magnesium may reduce Alzheimer's risk
- Incidence of premature ventricular beats and tachycardia is decreased
- Protects heart from oxidative stress, and post ischemic injury
- A useful adjunct to thrombolytic treatment
- Beneficial for cystic fibrosis
- Beneficial for both type 1 and type 2 diabetes
- Indispensible for proper neurological development and neuromuscular function
- Reduce migraine incidents
- No toxicity

Selenium

Selenium, a non-metallic element that is found in very small amounts in most animal species, is an important nutrient for maintaining health and vigor.

Claims:
- Antioxidant that keeps tissues and arteries elastic
- Decreases risk of clotting
- Boosts immune system
- Converts thyroid hormones to active form
- Most useful taken with vitamin E
- Protects against heart attack and stroke by decreasing stickiness of blood and thus clot formation
- Guards against cataracts and macular degeneration
- Promotes healing of shingles and cold sores (similar to lysine)
- Toxic level noticed by depression, anxiety, garlic odor

Oils: Krill, Fish, Flax, and Sesame

NOTE: Krill oil comes from small crustaceans that resemble shrimp. *It is not fish oil and will be allergy reactive for those responding to shellfish allergens.*

<u>Claims</u>:

- Reduces LDL
- Increases HDL
- Better concentration and memory
- Helps keep joints healthy
- Decreases signs of aging
- Promotes brain and nervous system health, function, and development
- Increases cell membrane protection
- Promotes liver health
- Gives relief for premenstrual symptoms
- Boosts immune system
- Aids mood disorders
- Encourages healthy skin and reduces skin damage
- Anti-arrhythmic
- Anti-hypertensive
- Anti-atherosclerotic
- Anti-inflammatory
- Cytoprotective and cardio-protective
- Prevents platelet aggregation
- Neuroprotective
- Reduce incidence of cardiovascular diseases including stroke
- Enhances nitric oxide production that produces vascular relaxation
- May protect from depression, schizophrenia, and Alzheimer's disease
- Lower blood pressure

Iodine

Brownstein (2009), in his outstanding book, *Iodine: Why You Need It* draws upon the work of Lugol, Abraham, and others to capture the fundamentals of how iodine impinges on health management.

The list of health issues associated with iodine deficiency that he has assembled is impressive, yet seemingly all but hidden from the consciousness of the medical establishment. Brownstein is among the very few authors I have noticed who not only can see his topic clearly but also recognizes parallel issues that need light. In this case, I refer to the fact that he clearly recognizes the role of dehydration in health management; otherwise Batmanghelidj, for example, seems to be out there by himself. ***Brownstein's description of the iodine breast cancer relationship deserves screaming headlines it seems to me. A must read for every adult female.***

For your convenience, here is Brownstein's list of conditions treated with iodine:

- ADD/ADHD
- atherosclerosis
- breast diseases
- Dupuytren's contracture
- excess mucus production
- fatigue
- fibrocystic breasts
- goiter
- headaches and migraine headaches
- hemorrhoids
- hypertension
- infections
- keloids
- liver diseases
- nephrotic syndrome
- ovarian disease
- parotid duct stones
- Peyronie's

- prostate
- sebaceous cysts
- thyroid disorders
- vaginal infections

Additional examples I have come across that may qualify are: insulin resistance, hearing loss, and stroke. Infections affected by iodine include bacteria, yeast, fungi, parasites, and viruses.

GLOSSARY

Agglutinating: Causing substances, such as bacteria, to clump together.

Allergen: A substance, such as pollen, that causes an allergy.

Atherosclerosis: Atherosclerosis is a specific type of arteriosclerosis, but the terms are sometimes used interchangeably. Atherosclerosis refers to the buildup of fats in and on your artery walls (plaques), which can restrict blood flow. These plaques can also burst, causing a blood clot. Although atherosclerosis is often considered a heart problem, it can affect arteries anywhere in your body. Atherosclerosis is a preventable and treatable condition.

Atrial Fibrillation: Atrial fibrillation (AF or A-fib) is the most common cardiac arrhythmia (abnormal heart rhythm) and involves the two upper chambers of the heart.

BIA: Bioelectric impedance analysis, or BIA, is a technique to estimate body composition based on the difference in electrical conductive properties of various tissues.

Blood-brain barrier: The blood-brain barrier (BBB) is a cellular and metabolic barrier located at the capillaries in the brain that alters permeability, restricting the passage of some chemicals.

Brain plasticity: Brain plasticity is a term used to refer to the brain's unique ability to constantly change, grow, and remap itself over the course of a lifetime.

Cardioembolic Stroke: The traditional definition of stroke, devised by the World Health Organization in the 1970s, is a "neurological deficit of cerebrovascular cause that persists beyond 24 hours."

Cerebral Ischemia: Brain ischemia, also known as cerebral ischemia, is a condition in which there is insufficient blood flow to the brain to meet metabolic demand. This leads to poor oxygen.

Chemotaxis: Any cell motion that is affected by a chemical gradient in a way that results in net propagation of a chemo attractant.

Childhood epilepsies: A recurrent disorder of the nervous system, characterized by seizures of excessive brain activity that cause mental and physical dysfunction, such as convulsions, unconsciousness, etc.

Chronic inflammatory demyelinating polyneuropathy: Chronic inflammatory demyelinating polyneuropathy (CIDP) is an acquired immune-mediated inflammatory disorder of the peripheral nervous system.

Clonus: Alternate involuntary muscular contraction and relaxation in rapid succession.

Collagens: The fibrous protein constituent of bone, cartilage, tendon, and other connective tissue.

Dermatomyositis: A muscle disease characterized by inflammation and a skin rash. It is a type of inflammatory myopathy.

Embolic Event: An embolism is an obstruction in a blood vessel due to a blood clot or other foreign matter that gets stuck while traveling through the bloodstream.

Endorphins: Any of several peptides secreted in the brain that have a pain-relieving effect like that of morphine.

Fibrinogen: A protein produced by the liver that helps stop bleeding by helping blood clots to form.

Foot drop: Paralysis or weakness of the dorsiflexor muscles of the foot and ankle, resulting in dragging of the foot and toes.

Guillain-Barre syndrome: A disorder in which the body's immune system attacks part of the peripheral nervous system.

HBA1C: The A1C test (also known as HBA1C glycated hemoglobin or glycosylated hemoglobin) is a good general measure of diabetes care. While conventional home glucose monitoring measures a person's blood sugar at a given moment, the A1C test indicates a person's average blood glucose level over the past few months.

Hemi paresis: Weakness on one side of the body. Contrast with hemiplegia, which is total paralysis of the arm, leg, and trunk on the same side of the body.

High-density lipoprotein (HDL): A type of lipoprotein that protects against coronary artery disease.

High Glycemic: High-glycemic foods are those that rate high on the glycemic index, a measure of the expected effects of different carbohydrate levels on blood glucose.

Histamine: An organic nitrogen compound involved in local immune responses, as well as regulating physiological function in the gut and acting as a neurotransmitter.

Hypoglycemia: An abnormally low level of glucose in the blood. Below-normal levels of blood glucose can be quickly reversed by administration of oral or intravenous glucose.

Immune globulin: A class of proteins produced in lymph tissue in vertebrates and that function as antibodies.

Inclusion-body myositis (IBM): An inflammatory muscle disease, characterized by slowly progressive weakness and wasting of both distal and proximal muscles.

INR: International Normalized Ratio. The prothrombin time (PT) and its derived measures of prothrombin ratio (PR) and international normalized ratio (INR) are measures of the extrinsic pathway of coagulation. It is a measure of how quickly blood clots.

Insulin resistance (IR): A physiological condition where the natural hormone insulin, becomes less effective at lowering blood sugars. The resulting increase in blood glucose may raise levels outside the normal range and cause adverse health effects.

Lacunar: Lacunar stroke or lacunar infarct (LACI) is a type of stroke that results from occlusion of one of the penetrating arteries that provides blood to the brain's deep structures.

Lambert-Eaton myasthenia syndrome: (Also called Eaton-Lambert syndrome.) A rare disorder affecting the muscles and nerves. LEMS is known to be associated with small-cell lung cancer. It may also be associated with cancers such as lymphoma or non-Hodgkin's.

LDL: Refers to low-density lipoprotein. Also sometimes called "bad" cholesterol. Lipoproteins are made of fat and protein. They carry cholesterol, triglycerides, and other fats, called lipids, in the blood to various parts of the body.

Multifocal motor neuropathy: A rare condition in which the muscles in the body become progressively weaker over months to years.

Multiple sclerosis (MS): A nervous system disease that affects the brain and spinal cord. It damages the myelin sheath, the material that surrounds and protects the nerve cells.

Myasthenia gravis: An autoimmune neuromuscular disease characterized by recurring muscle weakness and fatigue.

NINDS: National Institute of Neurological Disorders and Stroke.

Optic neuritis: Inflammation of the optic nerve that may cause a complete or partial loss of vision.

OSHA: Occupational Safety and Health Administration. A government agency in the Department of Labor to maintain a safe and healthy work environment.

Osmolality: A test that measures the concentration of all chemical particles found in the fluid part of blood.

OTC: Over-the-counter drugs.

Paraproteinemic IgM: Demyelinating polyneuropathy; chronic demyelinating polyneuropathy with benign IgM anti-myelin.

Polymyositis: A relatively uncommon inflammatory disease that leads to significant muscle weakness.

Pro Time: Prothrombin time (PT) is a blood test that measures how long it takes blood to clot. A prothrombin time test can be used to check for bleeding problems. PT is also used to check whether medicine to prevent blood clots is working.

Pro-arrhythmic: A chemical, drug, or food that promotes cardiac arrhythmias.

Raynaud's syndrome: A condition in which the smallest arteries that bring blood to the fingers or toes constrict (go into spasm) when exposed to cold or from an emotional upset. The small veins are usually open, so the blood drains out of the capillaries. The result is that the fingers or toes become pale, cold, and numb.

Stiff-man syndrome: A chronic progressive disorder of uncertain etiology that is characterized by painful spasms and increasing stiffness of the muscles.

TENS Unit: Transcutaneous electrical nerve stimulation, small devices that ease chronic pain by blocking pain signals using electrical stimulation.

Thromboembolism: The blocking of a blood vessel by a blood clot dislodged from its site of origin.

TIA: Transient ischemic attack. (Spelled ischæmic in British English; abbreviated as TIA, often colloquially referred to as "mini stroke") is a change in the blood supply.

tPA: Tissue plasminogen activator is a thrombolytic agent (clot-busting drug). It is approved for use in certain patients having a heart attack or stroke.

Viremia: The presence of viruses in the bloodstream.

Wolff-Parkinson-White syndrome: A condition characterized by abnormal electrical pathways in the heart that cause a disruption of the heart's normal rhythm (arrhythmia).

REFERENCES .

Achterberg, J. *Imagery in Healing*. Boston, MA: New Science Library, 1985.

Adams, J. "Biological Half–Life of Vitamin B12 in Plasma." *Nature* 198, (1963). 200 doi10.1038/198200a0.

Amen, D. *Change Your Brain, Change Your Life*. Three Rivers Press, New York, NY, 1998.

American Heart Association Information Sheet, *Live and Learn*. Retrieved on 3/16/10 from *http://americanheart.mediaroom.com/index.php?s=43&item=488*.

Apfalter, P. (2006). "Chlamydia, pneumoniae, stroke, and serological associations." *Strokes 2006*, 37:756–758

Appleton, N. *Lick the Sugar Habit*. Avery, member of Penguin Putnam Inc., Garden City Park, NY, 1996

Armstrong, L. "Assessing hydration status: the elusive gold standard review." *J. Am. Col. Nutrit.* (2007). Vol.216 No. 5 5755–5845.

Bach, R. *Illusions*. Delacorte Press/Eleanor Friede, 1977.

Batmanghelidj, J. *Your Body's Many Cries for Water*. Global Health Solutions, Inc., Falls Church, VA 1972.

_____*You're Not Sick, You're Thirsty*. Hatchette Book Group, New York, NY, 2003.

Berginer V., et al. "Clustering of strokes associated with meteorologic factors in the Negev Desert of Israel: 1981–1983." *Stroke* 1989; 20: (65–69).

Bernstein, R. *Dr. Bernstein's Diabetes Solution: The Complete Guide to Achieving Normal Blood Sugars*. Little, Brown and Company, New York, NY, 2007.

Bhalla, A., Wolfe, C., & Rudd, A. "Management of acute physiological parameters after stroke." *Q J Med* 2001; 94:167–172.

Black, P., and Garbutt, L. "Stress, inflammation and cardiovascular disease." *Journal of Psychosom Res.* 2002 Jan; 52(1):1–23.32. "Age and Aging." Oxford University Press on behalf of the British Geriatrics Society (2008), 37 (5): 608.

Bots, M., et al. "Level of Fibrinogen and Risk of Fatal and Non–fatal Stroke." EUROSTROKE: A Collaborative Study among Research Centers in Europe. *J Epidemiol Community Health* 2002;56 (Supplement 1):i14-i18; doi:10.1136/jech.56.suppl_1.i14

_____"Incidence and Risk Factors of Ischaemic and Hemorrhagic Stroke." *J Epidemiol Community Health* 2002; 56:i1 doi:10.1136/jech.56.suppl_1. i1qqq.

Borczuk, P., Medscape.com article. *emedicine* /757370, 2009.

Brownstein, D. *Iodine, Why You Need It, Why You Cannot Live Without It.* Medical Alternative Press, West Bloomfield, MI, 2009.

Byrne, R. *The Secret.* Beyond Words Publishing, Hillsboro, OR, 2006.

Campbell, L., Kuo, C., & Grayston, J. "Chlamydia pneumonia and Cardiovascular Disease." *Emerging Infectious Diseases* Vol.4 No.4, Oct–Dec 1998.

Campbell, T. C., and Campbell, T. M. *The China Study.* Benbella Books. 2006. Dallas, TX.

Center for Agriculture and Rural Development, Iowa State University, Winter 2005; Vol. 11, No.1.

Chapenko S, Millers A, Nora Z, Logina I, et al. "Correlation between HHV-6 reactivation and multiple sclerosis disease activity." *J Med Virol.* Jan. 2003. 69(1):111-7.

Coutts, S., et al. "Silent ischemia in minor stroke and TIA patients identified on MR imaging." *Neurology* 2005; 65:513–17.

Crawford, J. "Alzheimer's Disease Risk Factors as Related to Cerebral Blood Flow." *Medical Hypothesis.*, 46:367–77, 1996.

_____ "Alzheimer's Disease Risk Factors as Related to Cerebral Blood Flow: Additional Evidence." *Medical Hypothesis*, 50: 25–36, 1998.

Crawford, J. and Fishel, C. "Growth of Bordetella Pertussis in Tissue Culture." *J.Bact.*, 77:465–474, 1959.

Crawford, J., Dayhuff, T., & Gallian, M. "Hog Cholera: Replication of Hog Cholera Virus in Tissue Culture with Cytopathic Effect." *Am. J. Vet. Res.*, 29: 1733–39, 1968.

Crawford J., and Dayhuff, T. "Hog Cholera: Preparation of a Hog Cholera Immunogen from Photodynamically Inactivated Virus." *Am. J. Vet. Res.*, 29:1741–47, 1968.

Crawford, J., Dayhuff, T. & White, E. "Hog Cholera: Safety and Protection Studies with Photodynamically Inactivated Virus." *Am. J. Vet. Res.*, 29: 1749–59, 1968.

Crawford, J., White, E., & Dayhuff, T. "Hog Cholera: Response of Pigs Vaccinated Under Field Conditions with Photodynamically Inactivated Hog Cholera Virus of Tissue Culture Origin." *Am. J. Vet. Res.* 1968.

Dalakas, M. "Intravenous Immune Globulin Therapy for Neurologic Diseases." *Ann. Int. Med.* May 1, 1997 Vol. 126 no. 9 721–730.

Durlach, J. "Magnesium and Aging." *Linus Pauling Institute of Oregon State University* Information Sheet (n.d.). Retrieved March 19, 2010 from *http://lpi.oregonstate.edu/infocenter/minerals/magnesium*.

Dyer, W. *The Power of Intention*. Hay House, Inc., New York, NY, 2004.

Einstein, A., Calaprice, A., & Dyson, F. *The New Quotable Einstein*. Princeton University Press, Princeton, NJ, 2005.

Elkline, M., Lin, I-F, Grayston, J., & Sacco, R. The Northern Manhattan Stroke Study. *Stroke 2000*; 31:1521–1525.

Etminan, M., "Risk of ischaemic stroke in people with migraine: systematic review and meta–analysis of observational studies" *BMJ* 2005; 330 : 63 doi: 10.1136/bmj.38302.504063.8F (Published 13 December 2004).

Fu, et al. "Mycoplasma pneumoniae: the mystery bug. Middle cerebral artery occlusion after recent M. pneumoniae infection." *J. Neurol. Sci.* 157(1):113–15. 1998.

Gage, B., et al. "Validation of Clinical classification schemes for predicting results from the national Registry of Atrial Fibrillation." *JAMA* 2001 Jun 13;285(22): 2864–70.

Gaspar, D. "Fibrinogen: a new major risk factor for cardiovascular disease—review article." *J. Fam. Pract.* 1994 39: 468–77.

Gerber, R. *Vibrational Medicine.* Bear and Company, Sante Fe, NM, 1996.

Giles, J., Blumenthal, R., & Bathon, J. "Therapy Insight: managing cardiovascular risk in patients with RA." *Nat. Clin. Pract. Rhumatol.* 2006 June: 2(6) 320–9.

Gonzalas-Gay, M., et al. "Rheumatoid arthritis: a disease associated with accelerated atherogenesis." *Semin. Arthritis Rheum.* 2005 Aug; 35(1) 8–17.

Gordon, R. *Quantum- Touch: The Power to Heal.* North Atlantic Books, Berkley, CA, 2002.

Grau, A. J., A., et al. "Influenza vaccination is associated with a reduced risk of stroke." *Stroke* 2005; 36:1501–06.

_____"Recent Infection as a Risk Factor for Cerebrovascular Ischemia." *Stroke* 1995, Mar; 26(3):373–9.

Griswold, W., Oberndorfer, S., & Stuhal, W. "Stroke and cancer: a review." *Acta. Neurol. Scand.* 2009 Jan., 119(1): 1–16.

Graveline, D. *Statin Drugs Side Effects and the Misguided War on Cholesterol.* Self–Published by: Duane Graveline, MD, printed in the United States, 2008.

Guillain-Barre Syndrome (n.d.), Retrieved on 7/18/10 *http://neurologychannel.com/guillain/causes.shtml*

Gusev, E., et al. "The circadian changes of plasma and blood viscosity, hematocrit in patients with ischemic stroke." *Zh Nevrol Psikhaitr Im S S Korsakova* 2008; Suppl. 22; 61–65.

Gutierrez J, et al. "Multiple sclerosis and human herpesvirus 6." *Infection.* June 2002. 30(3); 145-9.

Handel, A., et al. "Type 1 diabetes and multiple sclerosis: common etiologic features." *Nature Reviews Endocrinology* 5,655–664 Dec. 2009.

Hay, L. *You Can Heal Your Life.* Hay House, Inc., New York, NY, 2010.

Health Key Public Service Bulletin, *CDC Behavior Risk Factor Surveillance System.* (2007). Retrieved on 11/23/10 from *http:///www.cdc.gov/brss/.*

Hopking, A. *Esoteric Healing.* Blue Dolphin Publishing, Nevada City, CA, 2009.

Ignarro, L. *NO More Heart Disease.* St. Martins Press, New York, NY, 2005.

IRIS Trial, "Insulin Resistance Intervention after Stroke Trial." 2005. *JAMA.* 2000; 284: 412–14.

Jan's Diet for Myotonia Congenita (n.d.), Retrieved on March 15, 2010. *http:// accessfitness.com/mcdiet.htm.*

Jorgensen, L., et al. Association of Albuminuria and Cancer Incidence. *J Am Soc Nephrol* 19: 992–998, 2008.

Jubelt, B., & Agre, J.C. "Characteristics and Management of Postpolio Syndrome." *JAMA. 2000*;284:412–414.

Kaplan, M. "Cardiovascular disease in rheumatoid arthritis." *Current Opin. Rheumatol.* 2006 May;18(3) 289–97.

Kehoe, J. *Mind Power into the 21st Century.* Zoetic, Inc., Vancouver British Columbia, Canada, 1987.

Kelly G. "Insulin Resistance: Lifestyle and Nutritional Interventions." *Alt. Med. Rev.*2000 Apr. 5(2): 109–32.

Kelley-Hayes, M., et al. "Temporal Patterns of Stroke Onset." *Stroke,* 1995, 26:1343–1347, The Framington Study, 1995.

Kenney, W., & Chiu, P. "Influence of age on thirst and fluid intake." *Med. Sports Exerc.* Vol. 33 No. 9, 2001 1524–32.

Kernan, W. IRIS Trial, "Insulin resistance intervention after stroke trial." 2005. *clinicltrial search.org/insulin-resistance-intervention-after-stroke. JAMA.* 2000; 284: 412–14.

Khaw, K., et al. "Association of hemoglobin A1C with cardiovascular disease and mortality in adults." EPIC—Norfolk *Int J Epidemiology* 2006; Aug; 35(4): 1034–43.

Kofoed, S., Wittrup, H., Sillesen, H., & Nordegestgaard, B. "Fibrinogen predicts ischaemic stroke and advanced atherosclerosis but not echolucent, rupture–prone carotid plaques." The Copenhagen City Heart Study. *European Heart Journal*; 2002. Vol.24, issue 6, 567–576.

Krispin.com: Retrieved on November 10, 2010 from *http://krispin.com/magnes. html.*

Kubetin, S. "Insulin Resistance and Stroke." *OB/GYN News*, June 15, 2002.

Laino, C. "Albuminuria strongly associated with stroke risk neurology today." 18 June 2009–Vol.9–issue 12–p. 4–6.

Linus Pauling Institute of Oregon State University Information Sheet (n.d.). Durlach, J., Magnesium and Aging) Retrieved March 19, 2010 from *http://lpi.oregonstate.edu/infocenter/minerals/magnesium.*

Lipton, B. *The Biology of Belief.* Hay House, Inc., New York, NY, 2008.

Lipsitch, M., & Viboud, C. "Influenza seasonality; Lifting the fog." *PNAS* March 10, 2009; Vol. 106 No. 10 3645–46.

Mack, G., et al. "Body fluid balance in dehydrated healthy older men: thirst and renal osmoregulation." *J. Appl. Physiol.* Vol. 76, Issue 4 1615–23 1994.

Manz, F. "Hydration and disease." *J. Am. Col. Of Nutrition.* Vol. 26 No. 90005 5355–54315 2007.

Margolis, J., Freitas, W., & Margolis, L. "Hypothyroidism Mimicking Myotonic Dystrophy." *J. Am Geriatr. Soc.* Vol.21 1973 31–32.

McTaggart, L. *The Field–The Quest for the Secret Force of the Universe.* Quill-Harper Collins, New York, NY, 2002.

Mendosa, D. "Living with Insulin Resistance." *Mendosa .com/ir.htm. Nat. Rev. Endocrinol.* 2009 Dec.; 5(12): 655–64 2009.

Nurmohamed, M. "Cardiovascular risk in rheumatoid arthritis." *Autoimmune Rev.* 2009 Jul.8 (8) 663–7.

Ngeh, J., et al. "Chlamydia pneumoniae, and legionella in elderly patients with stroke." *Stroke* 2005; 36:259.

Nguyen, T., & DeAngelis, L. "Stroke in cancer patients." *Current Neurology and Neuroscience Reports* 2006; 6(3) 187–92.

Noh, Kyung-Min, et al. "Insulin-Induced Oxidative Neuronal Injury in Cortical Culture: Mediation by Induced N-Methyl-D-aspartate Receptors", *IUBMB Life*, 48: 263-269, 1999.

Ornish, Dean. *Love and Survival.* Harper Collins Publishers, New York, NY, 1998.

Partinen, M., (June 1995). *Journal of Sleep Research, Vol. 4*, pp. 156–159.

Pert, C. *Molecules of Emotion*, Scribner, New York, NY, 1997.

Phillips, P., Bretherton, M., Johnson, I., & Grey, L. "Reduced osmotic thirst in healthy elderly men." *Am J. Physiol.* 1985; 261.

Pibram, K. "Languages of the Brain: Experimental Paradoxes and Principles in Neuropsychology." Prentice-Hall, Englewood Cliffs, NJ, 1971.

_____ "Rethinking Neural Networks: Quantum Fields and Biological Data," Prentice-Hall, Englewood Cliffs, NJ, 1993.

Poehlmann, K. F., and K. M. *Chlamydia Linked to Heart Disease, Stroke, and Alzheimer's* (Copyright 2002–05). Retrieved on 11/10/2010 from *http:// ra-infection-connection.com/Chlaymdia.htm*

Powers, J., et al. "Rapid measurement of total body water to facilitate clinical decision making in hospitalized elderly patients." *The Journal of Gerentology Series A: Biological sciences and medical sciences.* 2009 64 A(6):664–69.

Reaven, G., Strom, T., & Fox, B. *Syndrome X: Overcoming the Silent Killer that Can Give You a Heart Attack.* Simon & Schuster, New York, NY, 2000.

Rodriguez, G., et al. "The hydration influence on the risk of stroke (THIRST)." *Neuro critical care* Vol. 10 No.2/ Apr. 2009.

Rolef, B-S. (1998). "Hypnotherapy Research Society" degree course (essay 11—The Human Brain).

Rundek, T. "Insulin resistance predicts stroke, vascular risk in non-diabetics." International stroke conference 2008.

Sabin, A. "The Puzzler in Polio Epidemics." *JAMA* 1947L 134 (9) 749–756.

Singh, R, Barden, A, Mori, T., & Bellin, L. (February 2001). *Diabetiologica.* (Vol. 44, No. 2).

Spence, A. *Biology of Human Aging.* Prentice Hall, Inc., Englewood Cliffs, NJ, 1999.

Squizzato, et al. "Thyroid disease and cerebrovascular disease." *Stroke* 2005; 36:2302.

Stennis, W., and Craft, S. *J. Neurol. Sci.* 2006; vol. 245 21–33.

Simonton, O., S. Matthews-Simonton, et al. *Getting Well Again: A step-by-step, self-help guide to overcoming cancer for patients and their families.* Bantam Books, Toronto, New York, 1980.

Stroke Belt, The (n.d.). Wikipedia. Retrieved on November 8, 2010 from *http://en.wikipedia.org/wiki/Stroke_Belt.*

Talbot, M. *The Holographic Universe.* Harper Perennial- Harper Collins, New York, NY, 1991.

Taylor, J. *My Stroke of Insight.* Viking Penguin Group, New York, NY, 2009.

Texas Heart Institute, Stroke Risk Factors (n.d.). Retrieved on July 6, 2009 from *http://www.texasheart.org/HIC/Topics/cond/strokris.cfm.*

Third Lung. Betterthanair, Evergreen CO. Retrieved on February 24, 2011 from http://www.betterthanair.com/

Thompson, R., & Barnes, K. *The Calcium Lie.* InTruth Press, Brevard, NC, 2008.

Tomlinson DR, Gardiner NJ. Nat Rev Neurosci. 2008 Jan; 9(1):36-45. "Glucose neurotoxicity."

Tompkins, P., & Christopher, Bird. *The Secret Life of Plants*. Harper Perennial, New York, NY, 1973.

Torkildsen Ø, Nyland H, Myrmel H, Myhr KM. "Epstein-Barr virus reactivation and multiple sclerosis." *Eur J Neurol*. Jan 2008. 15(1): 106-8. Epub Nov 27, 2007.

Tzourio, C., et al. "Case-control study of migraine and risk of ischaemic stroke in young women." Recherches, Epidemiologiques en neurologie et Path. *BMJ*, Vol.310, April 1995.

University of Maryland Heart Center Information Sheet, *Atrial Fibrillation and Stroke* (n.d.). Retrieved on May 29, 2010 from *http://www.umm.edu/heart/af-stroke.htm*.

Urbanek, C., Palm, F., & Grau, A. "Influenza and stroke risk: a key target not to be missed?" *Infectious Disorders* Vol. 10, Number 2, Apr, 2010, 122–131 (10).

Van Doornum, S., Jennings G., & Wicks, I. "Reducing the cardiovascular disease burden in rheumatoid arthritis." *Med. J. Aust.* 2006 Mar. 20; 184(6) 287–90.

Verduzco, L. & Nathan, D. "Sickle Cell Disease and Stroke." *Blood;* 2009; Dec. 10;114(25) 5117–25.

Verzijl, N., et al. "Age–related accumulation of Maillard reaction products in human articular collagen." Advanced glycation end products: a review. *Biochem. J.* (2000) 350, 381–87.

Viboud, C., Alonzo, W., & Simonsen, L., 2006. "Influenza in Tropical Regions." *PLoS Med* 3(4):e89.

Wilhelmsen, L., Svardsudd, K., Korsan-Bengtsen, K., Larsson, B., Welin, L., & Tibblin, G. "Fibrinogen as a risk factor for stroke and myocardial infarction." *The New England Journal of Medicine;* Vol. 311:501–505, August 23, 1984, No 8.

Williamson, M. *Blood Sugar Blues: Overcoming the Hidden Dangers of Insulin Resistance.* Walker & Company, New York, NY, 2001

Wolf, P., Abbott, R., & Kannel, W. "Atrial Fibrillation an independent risk factor for stroke": The Framingham Study, *Stroke* 1991 Aug; 22(8) 983–8.

World Heart Federation Information Sheet; *Stroke and Blood Clots.* March 18, 2010.

Zukav, G. *The Dancing Wu Li Masters.* Bantam Books, William Morrow & Company, New York, NY, 1979

Index

Made in the USA
Lexington, KY
29 August 2011